Sticky Habits:

**How to Achieve Your Goals without Quitting and
Create Unbreakable Habits
Starting with Five Minutes a Day**

Barrie Davenport

ISBN: 1539626946
ISBN-13: 9781539626947

Disclaimer

Your Free Gift

As a way of saying thank you for your purchase, I hope you'll enjoy *39 Power Habits of Wildly Successful People*. These are daily and weekly habits you can incorporate in your life using the Sticky Habits Method outlined in this book.

Download this free report by going to
http://liveboldandbloom.com/39-habits-lp

Also, please enjoy my free, three-part Sticky Habits Video Training Series to further support your habit work.

View this free video series by going to
http://liveboldandbloom.com/sh-videos-lp

Contents

About Barrie Davenport

Barrie Davenport is a certified personal coach, thought leader, author, and creator of several online courses on emotional abuse, self-confidence, life passion, habit creation, and self-publishing.

She is the founder of two top-ranked personal development sites, LiveBoldandBloom.com and BarrieDavenport.com. Her work as a coach, blogger, and author is focused on offering people practical strategies for living happier, more successful, and more mindful lives. She utilizes time-tested, evidence based, action-oriented principles and methods to create real and measurable results for self-improvement.

You can learn more about Barrie on her Amazon author page at barriedavenport.com/author.

Barrie Davenport

Preface

Every person has the wisdom and intuition to know what is best for him or her. Sometimes we simply need someone or something to coax it out of us, show us the skills, and hold our feet to the fire so we follow through. That's what I hope *Sticky Habits* will do for you—show you the lifetime skills of creating new habits, so YOU can take charge of your life and make the positive changes you desire.

Just a few years ago, I was fortunate to learn these skills for myself. I was in the throes of a professional crisis after I'd left my long career in public relations to launch my own online business. When I began the business, my efforts were scattered and unfocused, and I couldn't get enough traction to move my business forward to make a sustainable income. Today, I'm running a successful business and earning a great income—all because I discovered the powerful skills of habit creation. But it didn't happen overnight.

After many wrong turns and lots of wasted time and energy, I learned the key to my success as a blogger was focused commitment to daily writing—sometimes up to 2,000 words a day. This was a huge challenge and an entirely new daily habit for my life and schedule.

I was fortunate enough to work closely with habit master Leo Babauta of the highly acclaimed blog *Zen Habits*. Together we conducted a habit study and taught the skills of habit creation in online classes. I also teach the skills of habit creation in my own course called Sticky Habits (StickyHabits.com).

I applied everything I was learning, researching from experts, and teaching in my courses to my own practice of writing—building from a few minutes each day to my current daily practice of writing 1,200 or more words. I also used my habit knowledge to form many new habits, including creating courses, running, changing my diet, juicing, stretching, positive thinking, and meditating.

Now it's my pleasure to share all this information with you, so that you can master skills proven to solidify and sustain new behaviors, so they become ingrained habits. Much research has been conducted on how and why habits are formed, how to break them, and how to start from scratch with a new habit. Starting from scratch is what we'll work on here—learning how to create brand new habits you don't abandon after a few days or weeks. You'll learn a method to create sticky habits that will serve you for the rest of your life and for as many habits as you desire.

Introduction

We all have habits. Some are good. Some are bad. Many of our habits have been with us for a long, long time. Every morning, you wake up, stretch, brush your teeth, shower, read the paper, sip your coffee with a teaspoon of sugar, then head to work, following the same route every day. Every day you might also smoke a few cigarettes, eat too much junk food, spend hours in front of the TV, have too many beers, or bite your fingernails.

Habits shape how you spend your time and the pace at which you move. They impact your health, your relationships, your mood, your energy, and your career. Habits are choices you make from a menu of possibilities, and quite often you make these choices unconsciously. Whether you are aware of it or not, in any given moment, you are choosing how your day will unfold—what you will do next, what habits you will follow. As one day leads to the next, a lifetime of habits adds up, shaping who you are and where you end up.

Your habits help define your life, and most of the habits you have right now are habits that have been formed over a long period of time. Some are habits you do without thinking—like getting the mail, putting on a seat belt, or brushing your teeth. Even your ways of thinking are habitual. If you examine your own thought patterns, you'll recognize you repeat many streams of thought several times a day, every day.

Habits can be quite useful and are an essential element of your brain function. They can increase productivity and make the actual mental and physical process of performing the habit more efficient and often more rewarding. Think about the difference in energy expended when you do something automatically and when you have to think about it. Imagine if you had to think through all the actions you take every day from showering to driving your car. It would be exhausting.

Habit Formation

Many habits you learned from your parents when you were a child. You adopted these behaviors because you were first instructed to do so (or suffer the consequences), and over time they became integrated into your daily routine. As you grew to adulthood, you maintained these thoughts and actions without ever examining whether or not you really wanted them any more. Some habits you formed in childhood as a way of self-soothing or stress release, like thumbsucking or hair twirling. Later on when you outgrew these behaviors or received negative reinforcement, you replaced these actions with other habits—maybe some that are not so healthy or positive, such as smoking or overeating.

Perhaps you observed some of your adult friends with habits you wish you had, but you were never instructed or encouraged to do these things as a child. If you grew up in a family that valued exercise and healthy eating, then these good habits were instilled from an early age, and they come naturally to you. If you didn't, then you look at your healthy friends and wonder why you keep falling off the wagon with your fitness and diet efforts. It all has to do with your brain. Amazing things happen to your brain during learning. Your brain makes connections that create neural pathways, like grooves in the mud. When you repeatedly perform an action or thought, your brain learns this pattern of behavior and sets up a pathway.

This pathway is an efficient way for the brain to process the routine, forming a new habit. Once the pathway is formed and the habit set, it is difficult to get rid of it. That's why breaking bad habits is so difficult. In fact, the brain doesn't care if the habits you form are good or bad. If you feed the brain with repetition, habits will appear and set up residence. The more you reinforce the habit with repetition, even after it is formed, the stronger it becomes. So those early childhood habits are quite entrenched and cozy in your brain.

If you attach the habit to another routine (like brushing your teeth before bed) or reward the habit with positive feelings and cravings (watching TV for your entertainment), you are further reinforcing the habit. However, it's the repetition that ultimately makes a habit stick. Understanding habits and how they are formed is important in helping you begin to create new habits or break old ones. If you know how your brain works, then you can create the mental, physical, and emotional conditions that will support you in adopting positive new habits. You can be kinder to yourself and less judgmental about past failures at habit change.

Most of us jump into creating a new habit without any real awareness of how to do it successfully. By working with the way your brain works instead of against it, you will have a far greater chance of success. That's what you'll be doing with the work in this book. You'll learn a method for habit creation that not only changes your behavior—it also alters your brain to reinforce and cement your behavior.

Your Sticky Habit

You've made a great investment in yourself and your potential for creating sustainable new habits by purchasing this book and learning the Sticky Habits Method for habit creation. As you proceed through the book, I recommend you work on one small habit of your choosing in order to practice the method.

It's best if you set aside a full six weeks to learn the method and practice your new habit daily beginning the second week after you start. During the first week, you will plan and prepare for your habit work—you won't perform the habit at all.

You should read all of the information in Chapters 1–8 prior to beginning your habit work. When you begin working on your habit in week two, you'll perform the habit daily, beginning with five minutes a day, and slowly increase the time every week.

Once you learn the habit skills, you can replicate them over and over again to build new positive habits forever. When you learn how to form new habits that stick, you can literally recreate your life, one positive habit at a time.

Important Note

Please plan to have a journal available as you go through this book to make notes and observations, as well as for your habit plans and daily accountability.

As you work through the first few chapters of this book, you will need to complete the Sticky Habits Planning Worksheet. You can recreate the worksheet outlined below in your own journal, and write down your decisions as you read the material and prepare during the first week.

Sticky Habits Planning Worksheet

Chosen Habit_____

Planning Week Start Date_____

New Habit Start Date_____

Research Needed_____

_____

_____

_____

Habit Trigger_____

Specific actions to take immediately after trigger_____

_____

_____

_____

Habit Reward_____

Accountability System_____

_____

_____

_____

Probable obstacles and how to overcome them_____

_____

_____

_____

People to inform about your habit work (those who will be personally impacted by this new action)_____

_____

_____

Positive Reinforcement/Encouragement Plan (your personal system for getting positive feedback for your efforts)_____

_____

_____

_____

Daily Positive Affirmation (a statement or statements you create to affirm the inevitable success of your new habit)_____

_____

_____

_____

Barrie Davenport

Chapter 1:
The Sticky Habits Method

Everything you want to achieve, every dream or long-term goal can be broken down into a series of habits. If you want to lose weight or get more fit, there are many new habits you must adopt in order to reach your goal. If you want to build a business, write a book, or meet the love of your life, these all require inserting new repetitive actions into your daily and weekly schedule that become habitual.

All habits aren't necessarily attached to bigger goals. Some are simply positive behaviors you want in your life, like learning to meditate or flossing your teeth. Even dropping bad habits requires you to learn and insert a new, positive habit in its place. All these simple habits and larger goals comprised of habits involve the same basic steps. These steps are what I'll teach you here—the Sticky Habits Method for habit creation.

Now I'm sure you've tried to create new habits in your life before, and you probably failed at making most of them stick. That's no surprise. According to a *Journal of Clinical Psy-*

chology report, only 8 percent of us are actually successful at following through and accomplishing what we resolve to do at the start of the new year. Habit creation is hard, and it's even harder because most of us go about it in the wrong way. We don't know why we keep failing. We think it has to do with personal weakness, but most of the time, it doesn't. It has to do with a lack of knowledge.

If you were trying to build a house, and you thought you could construct it using glue, the house would fall. You might try harder to rebuild it, adding more glue, filling in more cracks, and using different types of glue to see what works best. But the house still falls—not because you aren't working hard, but because you don't realize house-building with glue never works. Or if you decided to build a house, but you just learned basic carpentry, then you aren't prepared with the skills and will likely fail.

If you want to create a sustainable habit, you need to know what works and what doesn't. You need to know why some people create multiple lifelong habits while most of us keep using glue. You need to start with the basics and work up to more complicated, difficult habits.

If you've been frustrated and critical of yourself about your inability to sustain habits, rest assured you are not alone. Most people have trouble with habits. And it doesn't reflect a character flaw or lack of discipline on your part. You just haven't learned the method to make them stick.

So let me give you a quick overview of the Sticky Habits Method, so you'll know what to expect as you proceed through this book. It's a six-step method, and each part is essential to your success in habit creation. I'll go into detail about all these elements in subsequent chapters, but here's a quick overview.

1. Plan.

You'll spend the first week simply planning and preparing to work on your new habit. You won't perform your habit at all. You can't launch into a new habit without defining some specific rules and plans for yourself that you must establish from the outset. Once these plans are set, you'll begin your habit work in week two.

2. Start Small.

Most people fail at habit creation, because they've bitten off more than they can chew. The habit is too difficult, and they can't sustain the energy and motivation. That's why you'll begin with an easy habit that you practice for just five minutes a day for the first week or so.

3. Use a Trigger.

Perform your habit immediately after a cue or trigger. A trigger is a previously established habit you do every day, such as brushing your teeth. You'll create a bond between your new habit and the existing trigger by performing your habit immediately after the trigger.

4. Define a Craving and Reward.

People who are successful at forming habits always crave some reward, both immediate and long term. During the planning phase, you'll establish what you are craving related to your habit and how you can reward yourself immediately after performing your habit.

5. Create an Accountability System.

You need to announce your habit plans to a group that will hold you accountable to following through on your habit work and will give you positive feedback when you succeed. Accountability creates the uncomfortable tension that motivates you to do the work.

6. Make Adjustments.

As you work on your new habit, you'll discover some of the plans you made in the beginning might not be working well for you. This doesn't mean you should stop your habit work, but simply begin to test other options and make changes accordingly without interrupting your work.

So those are the six basic elements of the Sticky Habits Method, and you'll learn more about each step as you go through the book.

Reminder: Part of your planning during the first week involves selecting a habit you'll work on beginning in week two through the remainder of the six weeks.

Chapter 2:
Choosing Your Habit

OK, you're ready to create a habit, so let's dive in, right? Not so fast. When we decide to create a habit, we're itching to start immediately, but it's not the best idea. By diving right in, you're skipping some vital steps that will get you started on the right foot and ensure your success. Planning and careful preparation before you begin working on your habit will help you avoid the pitfalls you've likely encountered in trying to form habits in the past.

It's possible to just start, but you'll be lowering your odds of success. If you want to learn the skills of habit creation, you need to NOT perform the habit until you finish the planning. By preventing yourself from doing the habit for this week, you'll build up anticipation and excitement for the habit, which will motivate you through the first week or so of performing it.

It's like putting a beautiful piece of chocolate cake on your kitchen counter and telling yourself you can't eat it for a day.

You stare at the cake with desire, salivating and anticipating the next day when you can finally eat it.

So please, hold off with your habit, and prevent yourself from beginning this week, and then when you're ready, you'll want to do it even more. In the meantime, I have plenty to keep you busy. Commit to doing the actions below for this week, and you'll be successful in getting your habit off to a great start.

1. Pick one small, manageable habit.

Choose a small habit that you can do easily and use for practice as you go through this book. I'll list some ideas at the end of this chapter.

2. Select a start date.

Pick a date to begin your habit that's one week from the day you begin this book. Write this on your calendar and your habit planning worksheet. For future habit changes, you can set the date yourself, but one to two weeks is a good waiting period.

3. Create a habit plan.

Use this week wisely and actually write down your plan as outlined on the worksheet in the introduction. Take this plan seriously—if you skip over this step, you're shortchanging your habit work. Go all in.

4. Find an accountability group.

You can use online forums, as well as a blog, social media, emails to friends and family, people at work, or any group of your choosing. If you have a significant other or close friends, ask for their help. It's hard to do this without help. Ask anyone else important in your life for their help. Promise to call them if you have problems or feel like quitting.

How to Choose a Habit

How do you choose your first habit? You might have a long list of habits you want to create in different areas of your life (work, social, health, passions, etc.). So how do you just choose one?

Remember, the Sticky Habits Method requires you work on one habit at a time. You will eventually form as many habits as you like, but just one at a time. Why is this important? Because as you will learn through this book, making a habit automatic requires your focus and commitment. You can't divide your focus and expect to be successful at building a habit.

So how do you choose your first habit? There's no right answer. You should choose the one that's right for your life. Here are some guidelines for choosing your habit.

Positive

You can use the Sticky Habits Method to replace negative habits with positive ones, but for now, let's keep it simple. Choose a positive habit to create from scratch instead of replacing a negative habit. Positive habits might include walking, yoga, meditating, writing, painting, playing guitar, etc.

Easy

If it seems hard, do it later after you've built the habit-creation skill. For now, choose one that seems easy.

Brief

Initially you'll practice the habit for just five minutes a day. That might seem ridiculously easy, but you need to start small and increase your time slowly in order to establish the habit. This is essential to your success.

Fun

Choose a habit you feel excited about and enjoy doing. It makes it easier. If you dread doing it, you'll find it harder. If you enjoy it, there will be positive feedback built in.

Specific

Don't say, "I'm going to spend more time with my kids," but rather say, "I'll read to my kids for five minutes before they go to bed, after they brush their teeth." Don't say, "I'll talk to my friends and family more," but rather say, "Walk with mom every morning, right after breakfast." Don't say, "Be more productive," but rather say, "Do my most important task for five minutes as soon as I get to work."

Popular Habits

In the Sticky Habits course I teach online, students tend to choose certain habits most often. Here are some of the popular habits selected, although you don't have to choose any of these.

Exercise

This is by far the most popular habit, but it can be a difficult one if you attempt too much. Start with just five minutes, and make it something that doesn't require going somewhere (like to the gym), as that adds difficulty. Walk, jog, do pushups, practice yoga, jump on a rebounder, but keep it to five minutes.

Healthy Eating/Diet

This is easily the second-most popular habit. Don't overhaul your entire diet or try to quit soda or junk food. Instead, once a day eat some veggies or fruit that you like, or add drinking a full glass of water in the morning.

Getting Up Early

This is another popular habit, but it's a more difficult habit, as feeling sleepy is not enjoyable to most people and many people will go back to sleep. Wake just five minutes earlier for the first week (then ten, then fifteen, expanding by five minutes each week). Expect to be tired, but just get up and start moving.

Writing

Prepare a clutter-free writing environment in advance, so you don't get distracted when it's time to start. Also think through what you want to write in advance. When it's time to do the writing habit, just do it for five minutes.

Learning/Creative Pursuits

Use the same tips as the writing habit—just five minutes, and prep ahead of time.

Following a Daily Routine

This can be a whole series of habits, so be sure you add just one small habit to your current routine (even if that routine only consists of waking up, at this point).

Cleaning/Decluttering

Don't clean or declutter your entire home. Just declutter/clean for five minutes a day, after the same trigger each day.

Meditating/Prayer

This isn't hard, if you do it for five minutes a day at the same time each day. Make it easy and enjoyable.

It's important to note as you go through this book, the habit itself isn't as important as your ability to succeed at learning the habit skills and ultimately to succeed at the habit.

Learning the skills of habit formation is the goal of the book, and you must practice the skills on an easy, enjoyable habit. Save your bigger goals and more complicated habits for down the road when you've mastered the skills.

Here's a list of habit ideas you can consider.

Meditate
Recite affirmations
Drink more water
Write
Paint/Draw
Connect with spouse/partner
Play music
Journal
Practice yoga
Stretch
Walk
Run
Do sit-ups
Do pushups
Lift weights
Eat a healthy meal/food
Rise five minutes earlier
Go to bed earlier
Clean/organize/declutter
Learn something new (art, language, instrument, craft)
Network
Make your bed
Track your spending

Reminder: Once you select the habit you want to work on as you go through this book, please write it down in your journal, along with a start date one week from today to begin working on the habit.

Chapter 3:
Habits You Should Avoid

We talked about how to choose a habit as you learn the Sticky Habits Method, but people often get confused about the habit they select. They have a habit in mind from the outset and really want to tackle it, even though it's too hard for a beginner. There are certain habits you should avoid as your choice for now, because you want to ensure success as you're learning the skills. Difficult habits make it harder to succeed and more likely you'll give up on the program.

When you learn a skill—and forming habits is definitely a skill—you start with the easy version of that skill, not the hard version. When you learn to ski, you go on the beginner's slope, not the advanced slope, or you might break your neck. When you learn carpentry, you learn to hammer nails and saw boards, not build a house on your first day—or the house might collapse.

So start with the easy habits and skip the hard ones for now. You can always tackle advanced habit skills later.

Here's the list of habits to steer away from as you work through this book.

Advanced Habits to Avoid for Now

Waking Extra Early

This is a difficult habit because changing your body's sleep patterns is difficult, and lots of people fail to be consistent about waking early. Also the trigger is an alarm clock, which is not a natural trigger in your daily routine. Don't attempt to wake an hour early. If you do choose this habit, wake up just five minutes earlier at first, then increase by five minutes as your body adjusts. Consider putting the alarm clock in a place where you'll have to get out of bed in order to turn it off.

Quitting a Bad Habit

Whether it's smoking, biting your nails, drinking alcohol, or criticizing someone, quitting a bad habit is one of the most advanced habits there is. That's because there are usually multiple triggers instead of just one, and you have strong urges to perform the bad habit, which are hard to overcome. It's not impossible but definitely not a beginner habit skill.

Thinking Habits

Habits such as changing negative thinking or dropping a worry pattern are difficult, because we're often unaware of our thoughts, and changing thinking is similar to dropping a bad habit. It's not impossible by any means, but this is not the easiest of habit skills. Later in the book, I'll talk about using positive thinking for support, but for now avoid this one as your main habit choice.

Habits that Take Longer than Five Minutes

Some habits can't be done in five minutes. For example, if you're revising a screenplay, you might be able to work just minutes, but if you have a deadline, then that won't be enough. You'll want to do more, and that's not ideal for the first habit. Instead, choose to do some journaling or write part of a blog post for five minutes.

Habits with Too Frequent or Too Infrequent Triggers

The best trigger for your first few habits is one that occurs exactly once a day, and one that is already in your daily routine. If you perform your trigger many times throughout the day (like checking email), it's hard to consistently remember to do the habit. If you do something only on weekends, or two to three times a week, that's not often enough to build the habit in four to six weeks. It would take longer and require a strong focus.

Habits with Inconsistent Triggers

Some triggers are not regular at all, such as doing the laundry—which might happen today, or it might not happen for a few days. If you aren't sure if the trigger will happen exactly once every single day, don't choose that trigger.

Habits with Triggers That Aren't Already in Your Daily Routine

Let's say you want to choose a trigger such as "after I do yoga," but you don't already do yoga every single day. That's not a solid enough trigger for your new habit. If you want to set an alarm for your trigger, but that alarm doesn't already go off every day, that's not a good trigger. Then you're basically creating two habits at once—setting the alarm and doing the new habit.

Habits You Dislike Doing

If you dislike running or meditation or mowing the lawn, don't choose those for this first habit. Choose something you really enjoy doing, so there's positive feedback built in. You can form the harder habits later, but for now, when you're just starting out, make it easy on yourself.

Habits You Should Choose

So what habits should you choose? Habits that are

- positive,

- easy,

- enjoyable,

- physical, and

- tied to a trigger that already happens in your daily routine . . . once per day, exactly.

Reminder: Don't get too hung up on your choice of habit for this program. The purpose of this book is to teach you the skills of habit creation, using a small habit for practice. You may have many other harder habits on your list, but just pick one simple habit for learning the method.

Chapter 4:
Selecting a Trigger

One of the least understood elements of habit creation is the idea of bonding a habit to a trigger or cue. A trigger is a previously established, automatic habit or action that comes right before you take action on a new habit. In fact, all the unconscious habits you've ever formed throughout your life are simply actions bonded to a trigger. We've repeated the sequence of triggered behavior so often that it becomes ingrained, automatic, habitual.

For example, when you go to bed at night, you might unthinkingly brush your teeth and wash your face. Taking off your clothes and putting on pajamas might trigger washing your face, and washing your face triggers brushing your teeth. When you drive home from work, you might have your mind on other things and the driving route is automatic. That's because the turns we take and other actions needed to drive home have become habitual—we've done them so often, they're automatic. Each stoplight or stop sign or other visual cue becomes a trigger that cues the automatic habit of turning or slowing down, etc.

When we drive somewhere new, however, it's not natural—we have to be conscious and aware of every turn and signal. But if we repeated the route a hundred times, then it would become habitual. So when you are trying to insert a new behavior in your life, it will be like learning a new route. You will be conscious of every effort until you practice enough for it to become automatic.

You can't rely on your memory to jumpstart your new habit—it must be consciously performed immediately after the trigger. As we keep repeating this trigger-habit sequence, it becomes more and more automatic. Soon it's a habit and doesn't require conscious effort.

Consistency with your trigger/habit practice is important. If you do the habit right after the trigger, every single time, you're creating a strong bond. If, however, you sometimes do the habit after the trigger, and sometimes do something else that isn't the habit, then the bond is weak. It takes longer to create the habit if you're not consistent, and it's much faster if you're consistent.

In the book *The Power of Habit: Why We Do What We Do in Life and Business*, author Charles Duhigg discusses experiments in habit formation done with rats. He reveals that "the brain spends a lot of effort at the beginning of a habit looking for something—a cue—that offers a hint as to which pattern to use."

Here's what he learned from the rat experiments.

> From behind a partition, if a rat hears a click, it knows to use the maze habit. If it hears a meow, it chooses a different pattern. And at the end of the activity, when the reward appears, the brain shakes itself awake and makes sure everything unfolded as expected.
>
> This process within our brains is a three-step loop. First, there is a *cue*, a trigger that tells your brain to go into automatic mode and which habit to use. Then there is the *routine*, which can be physical or mental or emotional. Finally, there is a *reward*, which helps your brain figure out if this particular loop is worth remembering for the future.
>
> Over time, this loop—cue, routine, reward; cue, routine, reward—becomes more and more automatic. The cue and reward become intertwined until a powerful sense of anticipation and craving emerges. Eventually, whether in a chilly MIT laboratory or your driveway, a habit is born (p. 19).

The number of times you repeat this trigger-habit sequence is important. If you perform the trigger-habit sequence a hundred straight times, for example, you'll form a strong bond. If you've only done it ten times, the bond won't be strong. So smoking, as it is often done many times throughout the day, is an easier habit to form than, say, going running every New Year's Day, because that only happens once a year.

How to Choose a Trigger

For the first habit you tackle with the Sticky Habits Method, I recommend a daily trigger you already do exactly once a day, such as waking up, eating breakfast, brushing your teeth, arriving at work, putting your kids to bed, driving home, etc. If you pick a trigger you do less than once a day—something that you only do on weekends, or sporadically during the week, or every two or three weeks—then the trigger won't happen often enough for you to form the trigger-habit bond.

If you pick a trigger you do more than once a day and perform the habit every time you encounter the trigger (like forming the habit of drinking water every time you take a short break at work), then you'd form the trigger-habit bond faster than you would with a once-a-day trigger. But you'd also have to be conscious of performing the habit every time the trigger comes up, which means you need a laser focus on your new habit every single day, all day, for at least a couple of weeks. That's doable, but much more difficult than a once-a-day trigger—and, for now, we're sticking with the easier habit changes.

So pick a trigger you do exactly once a day and preferably at about the same time each day (it doesn't have to be exact). Think about your days, which might vary a great deal in routine. Some people have a regular routine, others don't. But we all do at least a few things regularly. For example, most people brush their teeth, shower, prepare food, eat a meal, etc.

I'd recommend choosing a trigger earlier in the day, as I've found it tends to be a bit easier. Later in the day all kinds of things come up that might interrupt the habit change, but early in the day is often less chaotic.

One last note—some triggers might be daily, but only on the weekdays—things like getting ready for work, commuting to work, etc. Those are fine, though slightly less ideal than the triggers you perform every single day. If you choose a weekday trigger, you'll just focus on the habit during the week, and give yourself a break on weekends. I'd recommend doing this for your second or third habit, but it's okay to do it for your first.

Spend some time carefully thinking about your chosen trigger for this book. You may decide down the road to change your trigger, if you find it's not working well for you, but it's best if you can select a trigger that has longevity and that occurs daily.

Here is a list of possible triggers to review to help you make your decision.

Waking up
Going to the bathroom
Brushing your teeth
Washing your face

Weighing yourself
Practicing daily prayer/devotional/meditation
Exercising
Showering
Walking the dog
Drinking water
Getting dressed
Making coffee/tea
Driving to work
Arriving at work
Taking your work break
Preparing breakfast/lunch/dinner
Eating breakfast/lunch/dinner
Turning on the computer
Checking emails
Getting in your car
Dropping off your kids
Feeding your pet
Putting the kids to bed
Arriving at your desk
Getting into your pajamas
Getting into bed
Arriving home after work
Taking your pills/vitamins
Getting the mail/newspaper

Reminder: Once you select your trigger, be sure to write it down in your journal.

Chapter 5:
Cultivating Cravings and
Establishing Rewards

Imagine this—you're sitting in an important meeting, and you feel the vibration of your phone letting you know a text has come in. You can't check your phone in the middle of the meeting, because you have an important client in the room. Then the phone vibrates a few more times during the meeting—more texts coming in.

Sitting alone in your office or at home or even in the car, when you hear a text come in, you immediately look at it. Satisfaction guaranteed. But right now, you can't look at your phone, and the longer you wait, the more you want to look at it. You crave looking at the phone, and every time it vibrates, the craving gets stronger.

You've probably known people who have had a smoking or alcohol addiction. Before they became addicted, just seeing a pack of cigarettes or a cocktail didn't make them want to smoke or drink. They didn't crave alcohol or cigarettes just by thinking about them. They began smoking or drinking in some setting, experienced the positive effects (the head-rush, the relaxation, the camaraderie with other smokers or drinkers, etc.). So they did it again and again.

Over time, with enough repetitive actions, just the sight of a cigarette or drink is enough for someone who's experienced the pleasure of smoking or drinking to crave satisfaction. If he or she doesn't get the smoke or the drink right away, the cravings become stronger.

Scientists have studied the brains of alcoholics and addicted smokers and have seen how their brain structure actually changes as their cravings become more and more ingrained. They've practiced that trigger/habit/reward system enough times that they are mentally (and physically) addicted, and their brains and behaviors are on autopilot.

This phenomenon isn't true only for unhealthy habits. Studies have been conducted on people who habitually exercise. In a 2002 study at New Mexico State University, researchers looked at 266 people who exercised at least three times a week. They began their exercise routines (running or lifting weights) more on a whim, as a way to deal with stress or to enjoy their free time. However, as they continued with repetitive exercise for many weeks, what drove them to continue and make their routines habitual wasn't just the exercise routine. It was their craving for the endorphin rush and the good feelings (like accomplishment, self-confidence, etc.) they received after exercising—the reward.

However, just having a trigger and a reward aren't enough to make a new habit have longevity. You have to expect the reward and begin to crave the positive physical, mental, or emotional feelings the habit provides. Your trigger must not only kickstart your habit, but also it must be a trigger for the craving of the reward.

Advertisers are brilliant at compelling us to habitually buy their products by teaching us to crave the rewards. Just look at the marketing messages for some of your favorite products. Colas aren't just going to quench your thirst—they're going to reward you with imagined happiness, refreshment, and all kinds of positive feelings a can of soda shouldn't be able to do. Cleaning products reward you with a sense of fresh smells, a job well-done, a feeling of satisfaction that your house is sparkly clean. One of the most brilliant recent marketing efforts is for Poo~Pourri, a spray that prevents unpleasant odors when you use the bathroom. We're now being rewarded for a natural function with a product that makes our unpleasant smells magically disappear.

Advertisers are hoping (and spending millions of dollars) to ensure we become addicted to their products by craving the rewards they offer. Even sunscreen companies are trying to find a formula that gives a tingling sensation once you apply the sunscreen. Fear of cancer isn't enough—we need an immediate reward.

It's the craving that drives our habits—so figuring out a way to ignite a craving is essential to forming lasting habits. And to do so, you'll need to reverse engineer the process, so you can focus on those cravings right from the beginning. You need to attach a craving and reward to your trigger and habit.

Identify Your Cravings to Choose a Reward

To establish this necessary pattern, begin by thinking about things in your life you already crave. For example, you might crave a latte from Starbucks, a piece of dark chocolate, checking your emails, surfing the net, or a catnap during the day. Often these cravings can feel like small indulgences—like a cup of tea, a warm bath, or a ten-minute break to read your book in the middle of a workday.

If you have a life treat or behavior you already crave, then attaching it as a reward to your habit and giving it to yourself immediately after your five-minute habit work will supercharge your habit formation. If you're already craving something, then don't allow yourself to have it until immediately after you perform your habit as a reward. Be sure to choose a reward you only allow yourself one time a day. (If you're eating chocolate all day, it won't feel like a reward to have one after your habit.)

If you don't already have a craving you can identify as your habit reward, then choose a reward that can turn into a craving over time. Some habit students have created a daily habit calendar and given themselves the reward of putting a gold star on each day they perform the habit work. They come to crave seeing the days lined up with gold stars and can't bear to see an empty space—a physical reminder they didn't perform their habit.

Other ideas that might turn into a craving could be a back rub from your spouse or partner immediately after your habit work, closing your eyes for ten minutes, or enjoying a hobby, such as knitting or painting. You could allow yourself to watch thirty minutes of your favorite TV program. You can dole out episodes as a reward.

If you are someone who enjoys a clean kitchen before bed or likes to straighten your desk at the end of the day, and it gives you satisfaction, then use something like this as your reward. Just be sure the timing works with your habit practice plans. If the reward is something you already crave—all the better. If not, choose a reward that is enjoyable, can be offered every day at the same time, and that's motivating for you when you think about it. Hopefully it's something you will eventually crave. However, try not to reward yourself with a negative habit you eventually want to break—such as smoking a cigarette, overeating, or drinking alcohol.

You can be endlessly creative in structuring your rewards, but the key is to make them fun and enjoyable and to time them immediately after your habit when you start with five minutes only. Then, as you build up to longer amounts of time with your habit, add a brief reward in the middle if that works for your habit. If you notice you are getting bored with your reward or you aren't craving it over time, switch it up so you don't become immune to the positive reinforcement. Diversity and excitement are part of what makes something interesting and fun.

Here are some ideas for possible rewards.

Gold stars
Checking off a checklist
Marking a calendar
Listening to music
Reading a book/magazine/blog
Watching a TV show/movie
Taking a break/resting/napping
Indulging in a favorite beverage/food/healthy treat
Taking a leisurely walk
Telling someone/calling a friend
Sharing on a forum/social media
Posting your success on your blog
Doing a crossword/Sudoku
Reciting an affirmation
Playing with your children/pets/friends
Having sex
Going biking/swimming/running
Checking email or social media
Sewing/knitting/crocheting/crafts
Painting/drawing/pottery making
Stretching
Gardening
Having tea
A massage from your partner or yourself
A hug from a friend

Reminder: Once you select your reward, be sure to write it down in your journal.

Barrie Davenport

Chapter 6:
The Accountability Factor

Creating a system of accountability balanced with rewards is essential to the success of habit formation. The former creates a motivating tension that propels you forward even when things are difficult or boring. The latter provides the positive reinforcement and good feelings that make the effort worthwhile.

We experience subtle forms of accountability all the time. If you've ever worked out with a personal trainer or taken a run with a friend, you have created accountability. You don't want to slack off in front of your trainer or friend, so you get up, put on your shoes, and push yourself a bit harder. If your boss asks you and your coworker to write a report, you'll do your best work to ensure the coworker doesn't outshine you.

Accountability can be powered by integrity, fear of embarrassment, pride, or shame. Whatever the reason for using it, accountability works. It provides the element of discomfort to get the job done—to make something happen that might not have happened without it—or at least to do it better. By putting yourself out there in front of others, you are holding yourself accountable to their good opinion of you. You are setting the bar for yourself, and then jumping up to tap it when someone is looking.

But what about when someone isn't looking? How do you jump up and hold on to the bar to sustain new positive behaviors? The most powerful scenario for accountability is the one you intentionally create for yourself. This is the accountability that can support you through important, sustained self-improvement. When you are trying to make a positive change in your life—to create a habit or reach a goal—accountability can be your best friend. It's a friendship you need to fully embrace if you really want to succeed.

When you are consciously creating and nurturing a baby habit, you must set up an incubator of conditions in your daily life so your habit can thrive. Having accountability doesn't mean you lack willpower or self-discipline. Our brains simply can't support a new habit until it's strong enough to support itself, so we need the extra impetus of having others pay attention to our actions. It's one thing to tell yourself, "I'm going to write every day." It's another to tell yourself and dozens or hundreds of other people—and to ask those people to pay attention, to ask about your progress, and to hold your feet to the fire.

To properly strengthen your fledgling habit, your accountability system should be serious and highly motivating. Personal coach and author Steve Chandler tells the story of creating accountability for his weight loss goals. He wanted to lose twenty pounds. At a staff meeting, he announced he'd give everyone in the room (about ten people) $1,000 if he didn't lose the weight by his target date. He put $10,000 on the line to ensure he met his goal, and of course he lost the weight. Steve's story illustrates the seriousness of his determination to be the person he desired to be. If you don't create serious and motivating consequences, your accountability system won't work. Of course, your system of accountability should be measured against the difficulty of your habit. Steve Chandler is skilled at setting up big habits and creating bold accountability.

For your purposes, I encourage you to start by breaking down more difficult habits into smaller, more manageable actions. If you want to lose twenty pounds, perhaps you start first by creating a habit of some simple eating changes, rather than tackling a complete overhaul of your diet and fitness routine. So you don't need to put $10,000 on the line in order to start eating more broccoli. But you can create a system that is realistically aligned with your habit goals.

For example, you could do one or more of these ideas.

- Announce your new habit to family and friends.

- Announce your habit plans, successes, and failures on social media.

- Ask a friend to be an accountability partner who checks in with you daily.

- Set up a daily update about your actions on a blog.

- Have a partner work with you on the habit.

- Agree to do a difficult chore or task for someone if you don't follow through.

- Put a white board in your home for all to see, with your daily habit actions.

- Work with a personal coach and report daily to him/her.

- Create a mastermind group that shares your habit goal.

As you set up your personal system of accountability, ask yourself these questions.

- Am I serious about making this habit part of my life?

- Will this system truly motivate me to take action every day?

- Do the negative consequences of the system feel real to me?

- What is my backup plan if this system fails?

Creating a system of accountability provides a negative tension that stimulates action, and this must be balanced with the positive reinforcement of your reward. Your accountability system itself will provide some emotional reward when you announce your successes and get positive feedback. If you avoid daily accountability with your habit work, the odds are high you will give up before your habit is automatic. If you seriously want a new habit, create serious accountability.

Reminder: Once you select your accountability system, be sure to write it down in your journal.

Chapter 7:
Why You Should Stick to
Five Minutes

The five-minute rule for new habit creators is often confusing and frustrating. When we've started new habits in the past, we usually begin with the amount of time we believe the habit takes to perform it properly. If we decide we want to run as a new habit, we'll start running for thirty minutes in the beginning. Or if we want to write, we think we need to write a full chapter or a certain number of pages. If we decide to add more veggies to our diet, we think we must prepare a full vegetarian meal.

When I started a running habit, I made the mistake I'm sharing here. I started out running for thirty minutes because I thought I was an exception. I thought I knew everything about habit creation so I could skip this step. But within the first week, I developed an injury and the pain almost immediately impacted my enthusiasm. I had to quit running and wait nearly a month until I healed to begin again. If I'd started with five minutes in the beginning and worked my way up to thirty over a few weeks, I would have avoided an injury, maintained my motivation, and saved myself a lot of time.

The five-minute rule is deceptively simple. You will definitely be tempted to break it, but don't. This is especially important in the first week as you establish the routine of your infant habit. You need to practice your habit every single day, immediately after your trigger—for five minutes only.

Five Minutes. No More. Here's Why.

Five minutes overwhelms our negative thoughts.

We all have limiting thoughts that keep us from creating new habits. We believe we can't form a new habit because we've failed so many times in the past. We are stuck in inertia and feel overwhelmed by the amount of time we think we must devote to our habit. But the five-minute rule beats back those thoughts. You can do anything for five minutes—even if you aren't confident, feel lazy or overwhelmed, or just don't want to do it.

Five minutes is easy.

People often avoid new habits because they worry they won't have time to fit it into their schedules. But five minutes is—well—just five minutes. We all can find five minutes in our day to perform our habit without interrupting our schedule drastically. As you increase your time slowly, it doesn't feel overwhelming or like a huge change in your daily schedule.

Five minutes provides immediate success.

Being successful at the outset of your habit work is so important. You want to feel positive and accomplished right out of the gate. That's why financial advisors suggest paying off smaller debt before bigger debt. It gives you a great feeling. When you achieve seven days of success with your habit for five minutes a day, it will afford you self-confidence and pride. This will motivate you as you move on and add more time to your habit.

Five minutes maintains energy.

When you begin with just five minutes of habit work, you're conserving your energy. Sure, you could start by blasting out thirty to forty minutes a day. But you can't sustain that over time—you must work up to it. It takes more emotional and mental energy than you can imagine to insert a new behavior into your mind and your schedule. Don't blow all your energy in the first week. Spread it out.

Five minutes beats all excuses.

It's really hard to find an excuse to avoid a five-minute habit. Five minutes is just too short an amount of time to say, "I don't have time; it's too hard; I can't do it." There are some habits you work on that will never be longer than five minutes—like flossing your teeth or making your bed every day or drinking a glass of water first thing in the morning. You won't need to increase the time (nor do you need to start with less than five minutes), but you will need to consistently practice your habit daily after your trigger.

If you accomplish performing your habit for five minutes only the first week, you can move on to seven to ten minutes the second week. However, if you miss more than a day during the first week, go back to five minutes the second week. This holds true for any week—if you miss more than a day of your habit work, go back to the previous week's amount of time. You will be tempted to break this rule, but if you do, your chances of habit success decrease dramatically. Incremental steps toward your goal are what determine habit creation.

Reminder: Don't increase your five-minute time too quickly. Add just five minutes more after the first week.

Chapter 8:
The Art of Preparation

Once you have determined your habit and selected a trigger, reward, and accountability system, you should be ready to begin working on your new habit. The day before or the day you begin your new habit, announce your plans to your accountability group. Also ask for support from your family or anyone else who might be impacted by your new behavior.

If you haven't made these decisions yet, please—don't begin your habit. Your chances of success are greatly diminished if you don't prepare properly. If you do have your plans in place, let's make sure you're completely ready to get started with your habit work. There's a bit more preparation you might need to do. On the day you get started with your new habit, and every day thereafter, you'll have certain steps to follow to maximize the enjoyment and success of your habit work.

Creating a new habit is like creating a work of art. Both require you to get your tools ready, arrange your space, mentally sketch your plans, and clear your mind before you begin.

Of course, your specific habit will determine how much preparation is needed on your habit days. If drinking a glass of water every morning is your habit, then you won't have much to do. But if you exercise, write, meditate, clean, organize, or any number of other habits, you may have a few things to set up prior to starting. Here are some thoughts to consider.

Your Tools

Just as an artist prepares the paints and brushes before he begins painting, you'll need to make sure you have all the tools necessary for your new habit. If your habit is running, make sure you have your running shoes and workout clothes clean and ready and easily accessible. If you want to write as your habit, make sure your writing program is pulled up on your computer or your favorite pad and pen are handy. If you want special items as part of your habit work (that is, your iPod for your run or a cup of tea when you're writing), be sure those are ready before you begin. Take time to think about the tools of your habit. Write them down and be prepared.

The Space

An artist generally has a studio in which she paints, and before she puts paint to canvas, she makes sure her space is properly appointed. The lighting is adjusted, the music turned on, the artistic subject placed just so. Consider the space for your habit work a sacred space, a space where you'll be creating yourself anew—just as an artist is creating a new work of art. Don't just begin your habit in any old room or space. Think carefully about where you want to perform your habit. What feels right and good to you?

If you run or walk, is there a lovely path nearby or place near your home for quick access (especially important during the five-minute days)? If meditation is your habit, find a calm and peaceful place in your home and arrange it as you want it on the first day you begin your habit. Decide on the lighting, the seating, and the temperature in the room. Have a backup plan for an alternate space for your habit work, in case something or someone gets in the way of your normal space. Interruptions and life changes are to be expected, so plan accordingly. In fact, think about what's happening in your life for the next few weeks that might interrupt or change your habit plans and consider possible alternatives.

Your Mind

An artist will spend time thinking about a painting or sculpture before he begins. He'll visualize the work he wants to create. He'll calm his mind and thoughts and allow himself to get into the creative flow. In the same way, prepare yourself mentally and emotionally to begin your habit work. Take a deep breath, clearing away feelings of stress or agitation. Sit quietly for a moment, and visualize yourself performing your habit. See the reward at the end of the habit. Watch yourself reporting your success to your accountability group. Smile as you think about your habit and embrace it mentally as fun and positive.

Remember, just as an artist is a creator, you are a creator of your own life by embracing and adopting new positive habits. You are adding beauty, texture, color, and vibrancy to your life, as you gain mastery over this new habit. As you begin your new habit work today or in the coming days, get started on the right foot by preparing yourself, your tools, your space, and your mind.

Reminder: Once you begin your habit work, complete the Sticky Habits Daily Habit Reporting Form (shown on the next page) every day. You can recreate this form in your journal, and complete the answers once you finish your habit or even if you miss your habit. This is your own personal accountability system.

Sticky Habits
Daily Habit Reporting Form

Date_____

Please fill out this form every day, right after you've done your habit. Try not to, but if you miss a day, fill out the form the next day for the day you missed and for the current day.

Did you do your habit today? ____yes ____no

Did you do your habit right after your trigger? ____yes ____no

Did you use your accountability system? ____yes ____no

If you didn't do the habit, why not?

_____

_____

Was your habit easy or hard today? ____easy ____hard

How do you feel today, either emotionally or physically?

_____

_____

What challenges or roadblocks came up?

_____

_____

Chapter 9:
Harnessing Habit
Launch Enthusiasm

You've spent a week planning and preparing to begin your habit. You've determined your trigger, set up accountability and rewards, and made sure you have everything you need to launch your new habit. You've made the decision once and for all to learn the skills of habit creation, and you are reading this book to make it happen. Now you've had to wait a week, and you're chomping at the bit to work on your new goal.

By reading the past few chapters, you've already learned a lot about how habits are formed and what you need to do to ensure they stick once you get started. In fact, you may feel you know everything you need to know to successfully create your habit. The enthusiasm you're feeling right now is a wonderful thing. If you could harness it and tap into it over the next five weeks, you *would* have everything you need to create a habit. When you're excited and motivated, you can achieve anything. But unfortunately, that enthusiasm doesn't naturally stick around.

Think about times in the past when you've tried to create a new habit. Often we do this as a New Year's resolution. This first week or so, we're off with a bang as we begin working on our resolution. But it isn't long before we end with a whimper. Our excitement and enthusiasm dissipate as we experience how hard it is to stick to our guns, day in and day out. We begin to make excuses to justify our desire to quit. Maybe we decide our loss of enthusiasm is a sign we just aren't meant to pursue this particular habit after all. It's impossible to feel enthusiastic about something we come to dread.

Even when you know the skills of habit formation, maintaining motivation and enthusiasm can be hard as the weeks go by. Initially you're carried by the tide of newness and anticipation about your new habit. But within a few weeks, the bloom is off the rose. That's why it is so imperative you stick to the Sticky Habits Method to help you through these more difficult times. Aside from sticking to the method, there are other ways you can harness the enthusiasm you're experiencing as you begin and spread the motivation over the next few weeks, as you are solidifying your habit.

Here Are Some Thoughts

Find a Buddy

Sharing your habit time and goals with another person is always more inspiring and motivating. Ideally, find someone who wants to develop the exact same habit as you, and do the habit work together. However, this might be hard to coordinate unless it's your spouse/partner or someone living with you or close to you. Instead, you could have a buddy you check in with before and after your habit work, and you each offer support and encouragement to the other.

Make It Fun

Do whatever you can to make your habit time fun. View this habit work as special time for you—a gift you are giving yourself. If it works for your habit, play great music while performing it. Light a beautifully scented candle, or practice your habit in your favorite room of the house. Brainstorm ideas for keeping your habit work exciting and interesting.

Stick to the Slow Time Increase

This can be hard, especially if your habit is something that will ultimately take a good chunk of time. But be sure to stick to five minutes in the first week and maybe the second week too. Increase the amount of time by a few minutes each week as your habit becomes automatic. By keeping your time manageable and easy, you'll be able to maintain your motivation and energy to pursue your habit.

Stay Mindfully Focused

Prior to performing your habit, try not to allow yourself to ruminate on it too much. Don't spend time dwelling on feelings of dread or resistance. When you are performing your habit, keep focused on the task at hand. Try to do the work of the habit without analyzing it or thinking about how you are feeling or how hard it might be. Stay in the present moment.

Stay Connected

Keep in contact with your accountability group, family members, and friends to communicate and share your experiences. This network of people can be your best resource for motivation and renewed energy when the going gets rough.

Remind Yourself Why

Every day, remind yourself of the reason you want to accomplish this habit. Imagine yourself as you will be once you have developed this new habit. Think about how you will feel. Embracing the reason for a goal keeps us emotionally connected to our daily work. Every daily achievement brings us closer to our imagined outcome, until one day a few weeks down the road, you can celebrate your success. We'll discuss this more in the next chapter.

Stay Happy and Positive

During the weeks you work through this book, do what you can to minimize stress, difficult decisions, and interpersonal conflicts. Simplify your life and activities, and consciously focus on gratitude and joy. Allow the beautiful, happy aspects of your life to move to the forefront of your thinking, so you can bask in positive energy as you work on your habit. Don't allow negativity to drain you of the energy you need to focus on your new habit.

As you begin your habit, you should be carried along on a wave of excitement as you get started. Enjoy this time and appreciate the ease of your habit work as you begin. Don't worry if your enthusiasm wanes over time—that's to be expected. You can take action to minimize your loss of enthusiasm and keep your motivation high. All the elements of the Sticky Habits Method will help you stay committed to your habit work, but enthusiasm and fun add fuel to your engine to accelerate your habit efforts.

Reminder: Be sure you complete your Sticky Habits Daily Habit Reporting Form and report to your accountability group.

Chapter 10:
Understanding the
Why of Your Habit

Throughout this book, I've talked about various techniques to make habit formation easier—keeping it small, using triggers, having accountability. But to fully embrace your new habit, it's good to hit the refresh button in your mind, and remind yourself exactly why you are doing this. What's so important about this habit? Why are you spending your money on a book to help you create it—or any future habit?

In my coaching practice, I frequently work with clients who aren't happy with their jobs or their lives in general. They feel lost and without passion or meaning in life. One of the first exercises I take them through is to define their most important life and work values. I give them a list of value words they must narrow down to their top five.

For success and happiness in any endeavor, it's critical that your choices and actions are aligned with these most important values. You know what it feels like when you are living outside your values. For example, if you value simplicity, but your life is over-scheduled and stressful, you aren't being true to your authentic self. This misalignment can manifest with anxiety, guilt, depression, anger, and a variety of other bad feelings.

The person you are, that you reflect to the world, is a collection of your habits and behaviors. Others measure us, and we measure ourselves, by those actions. Fortunately, we have the power to reinvent ourselves every day. You are doing that right now by tackling this new habit. It's good to remind ourselves during this process why we are doing it. Hopefully, you've chosen a habit aligned with your values. In doing so, you've chosen to express who you really are and what's most important to you. That's amazing and really bold, as many people try and fail at creating habits that reflect their true selves. You, however, have committed to creating your best self by embracing this new habit through your daily work.

So if you come to view your habit as an expression of yourself—one you are claiming and fully embracing—it packs the power of purpose and meaning into your efforts. You aren't doing this habit just because it seems like a good thing to do. You are doing it because it's part of you, and you want to love and nurture it completely. Why would you neglect an important part of yourself? Let's take a moment for you to focus on this idea right now.

Get your journal and pen, and write down your answers to the following questions.

- What personal values does your habit reflect for you? Write down the value words that come to mind. For example, if your habit is exercise related, you might write: fitness, energy, health, self-respect, integrity. You can find a list of 400 value words at http://liveboldandbloom.com/05/values/list-of-values

- What does your habit tell the rest of the world about you, especially those who see you as a role model?

- How will embracing this new habit make you feel about yourself? Write down words that reflect your emotions.

- Who will you be once you've fully adopted this new habit into your life? Write the answer to this, as though you are describing yourself the way a friend would now describe you.

- How will this habit make you more of the person you want to be? (Read the exercise below to help you define that person.)

I'd like to suggest you take your answers and post them somewhere you'll see them regularly. Maybe even read them before and after you do your habit. When you remember your habit has the purpose of self-creation behind it, it's much harder to blow off your daily work. If you want to dig a bit deeper, consider these simple exercises to help you define a vision for your ideal self, which in turn will help you know what habits are most important for you:

1. Sit down with your journal and write down the qualities of your ideal self, a self who embraces positive new habits. For example, "I want to be a person who is honest. I want to be a person who follows through on commitments. I want to be a person who solves conflicts without condemning or belittling. I want to be a person who lives simply."

2. Dig a little deeper and write some examples of how and when you will become this person. For example, "As an honest person, I will be true to myself and my own needs, as well as being genuine and trustworthy with others. In my effort to live simply, I will have fewer daily tasks so I can focus on them mindfully and completely." Find the places where you are farthest from your ideal and specifically define the actions that you aspire to.

3. Play the part of the character until it becomes natural for you. If you must pretend at first, then do it. Act "as if." For example, the next conflict you have with your partner or a friend, act as if you are capable of giving unconditional love and support—and then give it, despite their reactions, comments, or misunderstandings. Yes, it will feel false at first, but with practice, you will transform.

4. Rehearse daily and be a creator, not a reactor. Now that you have a character study of your ideal self, continue to create and express this person every day. You are the author of your life and your behavior. Don't undermine your vision of yourself just to defend your ego or hurt feelings. It's never worth it. Don't allow your initial negative reactions to a situation damage your new ideal self. Revisit your character study regularly, as a reminder of the role model you have created for yourself.

5. You can always revise and rewrite your ideal self. Because we are human, we fail and falter at being the who we want to be. But every day we have the opportunity for a revision. We can correct our course and step back into our ideal self. Along the way, we might want to adjust our vision to align with our personal evolution.

As we change and grow, we may want to expand our personal character study, adding more dimension, subtlety, and flexibility. So often we struggle to make everyone else conform to the "who" we want them to be. Think of the hours spent trying to script the behavior of others. But there is only one character in your life story whose behavior and reactions you can alter—your own. That's what you're doing with this habit work. Write the story of who you want to be. Create a character who could be a role model to others. Define the habits, responses, and values of this person. Then go live it. Before you know it, this new "who" will be you.

Reminder: Be sure you complete your Sticky Habits Daily Habit Reporting Form and check it with your accountability group.

Chapter 11:
Your Brain and
Habit Creation

Here's some good news about creating habits: if you alter your brain, creating new habits is a cinch. This doesn't mean you need brain surgery or mind-altering drugs. What it does require is that you repeat small behaviors frequently enough that your brain begins to carve out new neural pathways. That sounds complicated, but there is an entire field of science that recognizes and studies the brain's remarkable ability to mutate and grow. It's a revolutionary, exciting science called neuroplasticity.

Neuroplasticity shows that our repetitive thoughts and actions can change the structure and function of our brains. The idea was first introduced by philosopher and psychologist William James in 1890, but it was soundly rejected by scientists of the time who uniformly believed the brain was rigidly mapped out, with certain parts of the brain controlling certain functions. They believed that if a part of the brain was dead or damaged, the function was altered or lost altogether. It appears James' critics were wrong.

The science of neuroplasticity now enjoys wide acceptance, as scientists are proving the brain is endlessly adaptable and dynamic. It has the power to change its own structure, even for those with the severe neurological afflictions. People with problems such as strokes, cerebral palsy, and mental illness can train other areas of their brains through repetitive mental and physical activities.

Neuroplasticity is "one of the most extraordinary discoveries of the twentieth century," according to psychiatrist Norman Doidge, MD, author of *The Brain That Changes Itself.* Neuroscience demonstrates the brain is constantly forming new neural pathways, removing old ones, and altering the strength of existing connections. This means the brain is able to adjust and adapt physically at any age to compensate for an injury or illness and to adapt to new behaviors, situations, or changes in the environment. The brain is not fixed, but rather it's like clay—a malleable structure that molds itself in response to information and experience.

Rewire Your Brain

So what does this have to do with you and creating habits? It means repetitive thoughts and behaviors can rewire your brain to create new neural pathways that reinforce and cement a new habit. Every time you repeat a behavior, you are giving your brain a cue to recognize this behavior as automatic. For small, easy behaviors, the number of repetitions needed is less than bigger, more difficult behaviors.

If you add positive thinking and visualization to the repetitive behaviors, you are supercharging your brain's response to a new habit, helping it to form even more quickly. Jeffrey Schwartz, author of *The Mind and the Brain: Neuroplasticity and the Power of Mental Force*, made an extraordinary discovery while using the therapy he developed for his patients with obsessive-compulsive disorder. By actively focusing their attention away from negative behaviors and toward more positive ones, Schwartz's patients were using their minds to reshape their brains. They were effecting significant and lasting changes in their own neural pathways, using their mind to change their brain.

A further application of this discovery is the use of visualization to change the brain. A review in the *Strength and Conditioning Journal* describes how to use imagery to improve strength training. One study detailed how novice weightlifters visualized a bicep-curl exercise three times a week for eight weeks. The participants did not actually do any bicep curls or any other elbow-flexion exercise during that time. However, they still gained strength in both the elbow flexors and extensors (44 and 32 percent increase in strength, respectively). The body recognizes the brain's signals even without physical action.

World-class athletes use visualization regularly to enhance performance and optimize the possibilities for success. But these techniques don't have to be limited to the psychologist's office, science lab, or the world of sports. They can be used by everyone, all the time, in our efforts to change our thoughts and behaviors and ultimately to create more satisfying lives.

Imagine this—every time you work on creating a new habit, your brain is being rewired. New connections are forming and old ones are losing their potency. The recent connections created by new habits are strengthening, and those you no longer need are disappearing. With your brain's remarkable ability to change, every day and every moment you have the capacity to reinvent yourself. By consciously choosing your actions and reinforcing them with repetition, positive thinking, and visualization, you have the power to create new habits for life.

If you want to reinforce your brain's efforts on behalf of your brand new habit, here are some action steps.

- Once you determine the habit your wish to create, write down three positive affirmations that support this new habit. For example, if your habit is walking every day, an affirmation could be, "I look forward to my daily walk, and it is easy for me to incorporate it into my day."

- Whenever you feel resistance or have negative thoughts about your habit, repeat your affirmations out loud or say them silently to yourself. This will feel awkward at first, but you are training your brain to embrace this new habit.

- Take a few minutes twice a day to visualize yourself doing this new habit. Mentally reinforce the physical action you want to take.

Continue to consistently perform your habit. Adopting a new habit requires repetition, repetition, repetition. That's what your brain needs in order to throw out the welcome mat for your habit. Remember that easier habits will take less time to become automatic than will more difficult habits. Be patient with yourself, as you wait for your brain to catch up with your new habit.

Reminder: Be sure you complete your Sticky Habits Daily Habit Reporting Form and report to your accountability group.

Barrie Davenport

Chapter 12:
How Long Does It Really Take to Create Habit?

In 1960, Dr. Maxwell Maltz published a best-selling book called *Psycho-Cybernetics* in which he discussed his observations about how long it took amputees to adjust to the loss of a limb. He found it took them twenty-one days on average and therefore concluded that twenty-one days is the magic number for habit creation. His book became a blockbuster hit, selling more than thirty-five million copies.

However, Dr. Maltz's book perpetuated a myth about the length of time it takes to make a new habit automatic—a myth that has lasted for years. The twenty-one-day rule simply doesn't apply to everyone or even to most people. The truth is, the amount of time it takes to create a habit depends on the habit and the habit creator.

In a 2009 study published in the *European Journal of Social Psychology*, Phillippa Lally and her colleagues from University College London conducted more definitive research on habit creation. They recruited ninety-six people wanting to form a new habit, like eating a piece of fruit with lunch or running for fifteen minutes each day.

The participants were asked each day how automatic their chosen habit felt after performing it. On average, they found their habit to be automatic in sixty-six days. So in general, it can take a little more than two months before a new habit really becomes a habit. However, this is a general rule of thumb and can vary widely depending on the habit, the person performing the habit, and the circumstances. For some people, it took only eighteen days. Others took as long as 254 days to form the habit.

In fact, your choice of a new habit profoundly impacts the amount of time it takes for it to become automatic. In Dr. Lally's study, those who chose drinking a glass of water daily reached their habit goal much more quickly than those attempting the habit of doing fifty sit-ups a day. That's why I suggest you work on a simple habit during this program. You will learn the skills of habit creation while enjoying relatively rapid success in making your habit automatic.

The important factor in either simple or difficult habits is repetition. Although Dr. Lally's study found that missing just a single day of habit practice during the twelve-week study didn't reduce the chance of success, it's those early repetitions that give us the boost in making the habit stick. Staying on track as much as possible will definitely help you reach your habit goals more quickly.

Before you get discouraged about the amount of time it takes to create a habit, please remember that habits are hard to create. That's why so many people fail at creating them and why you are reading this book. Many people underestimate the time it takes and build their expectations around the twenty-one-day myth. That alone is enough to throw you off track.

Having realistic expectations from the outset will help you manage your emotions and frustrations during the process. In the scheme of things, spending several months to form a valuable habit is nothing in the span of your entire life. We waste so much of our time on invaluable activities every day, like watching TV or surfing the net—so why not use our time on something far more productive and life-altering, even if it takes a few months?

Also remember that Dr. Lally's study did not incorporate many of the elements of the Sticky Habits Method. Although the participants did perform their habit after a trigger, there was no system of rewards, little preplanning, and slight accountability beyond reporting their daily efforts on a questionnaire. Nor were the participants asked to stick to the five-minute rule.

One habit we've all unconsciously adopted is the mindset of expecting immediate results. We want quick solutions and immediate answers, because so much information comes to us at lightning speed. We've lost the art of patience and the appreciation of process.

New habits do take time. But every small success along the way is a gift, and every failure is a lesson. With commitment to the process and understanding that occasional failure doesn't mean you're incapable, you WILL reach your habit goal. There is a pot of gold at the end of the habit work rainbow.

Practice your habit daily. Enjoy the process. Share your experiences. Reward yourself for small successes. Forgive yourself for small failures. Have a mindset of enthusiastic expectation. Not only will you reap the rewards of a positive new habit, but you'll also experience the joys of learning, stretching yourself, and daily small accomplishments.

Reminder: Be sure you complete your Sticky Habits Daily Habit Reporting Form and report to your accountability group.

Chapter 13:
Overcoming Emotional Barriers to Habit Success

As you begin to work on a new habit, you want to be in the right frame of mind with a sense of positive expectation, focus, and self-confidence. When you feel strong emotionally, you will be more successful at creating habits. Sometimes this just takes a subtle shift in your awareness to get emotionally prepared to take on a new habit. You take time to clear away mental and physical distractions, so you have plenty of positive emotional energy to give to this new endeavor. Then you use this energy to support your fledgling habit.

You can do this with specific mental exercises, such as positive thinking and affirmations. These exercises don't just make you feel better. If repeated regularly, they alter the neural pathways in your brain, making it easier for the new habit to take hold. However, if you're really struggling with your emotions, you're starting out on the wrong foot and expending energy that should go toward your habit work. The odds are greater you will slip into negative thinking patterns that will undermine any of the physical habit work you're doing. So it's important to take a good look at your emotional state before you begin. If you address and clear up these emotions first, you will greatly increase the likelihood of forming a life-long habit.

Sometimes we aren't aware of our emotional state or what's at the root of our feelings. We may feel anxious, stressed, angry, sad, or out-of-sorts, but we aren't sure why. Awareness is the place to start. You wouldn't begin a race if you felt ill. You'd wait until you got better, and you'd address what was wrong. You don't want to begin a habit if you feel emotionally under the weather.

So how about you—can you identify how you are feeling now? If you are generally feeling upbeat and positive, that's great. But it's worth doing a little digging to make sure. As you review the following questions, take a minute to close your eyes and think carefully about what comes up for you. You may need to take a moment between questions so you can write down your answers in your journal. First, take about eight deep breaths to relax your mind and body.

Here Are the Questions

1. What is your current emotional state right now, as you are sitting in your chair? If you have several emotions, write them down in your journal.

2. For each emotion, ask yourself, "Why am I feeling this way?" Keep asking "why" for each answer until you run out of answers. For example, you might say, "I'm feeling stressed because I have too much work do. Why? Because I've taken on too much? Why? Because I can't say no. Why? Because I don't create boundaries for myself." You see how I carry this on until I reach a deeper and deeper cause for the feeling. Be sure to write down your answers.

3. What has been your emotional state during the past few weeks? Do you have any long-lasting feelings of sadness, anxiety, or stress? If so, go through the same exercise of asking yourself why you have been feeling this way.

4. Next you want to address these emotions. First, look at your current emotions and the causes you listed. Are there some specific actions you can take to deal with these issues? Write down some of the actions you can take and when you can take them. By addressing even a few of these situations, you will be lightening your emotional burden, making it easier for you to create a new habit.

If you have negative emotions that have been hanging on for quite a while, you may need some support from a coach or counselor to address these before you begin the challenge of starting a new habit. If you are potentially depressed, anxious, or going through a difficult life challenge, this may not be the best time to create a new habit. Clear up the emotions first, so that you lay a solid foundation for success.

Even if you aren't ready to begin your habit, this book will give you the tools you need when you are. By learning about how to create a habit, you are empowering yourself, which often helps in healing negative emotions. To prepare for a successful new habit, prepare yourself emotionally first. Clear up any issues that are weighing you down, so that you can focus your energy on your positive new habit.

Reminder: Be sure you complete your Sticky Habits Daily Habit Reporting Form and report to your accountability group.

Chapter 14:
Creating Positive and
Negative Feedback

During the weeks of practicing your habit, it's helpful to arrange your life in a way that supports your habit success. Setting up both positive and negative consequences in your daily life is a great way to help you stay on track. In his ebook about changing habits, blogger Scott Young (www.ScottHYoung.com/blog) describes the process of forming habits like walking home through fresh snow. The first person to walk through the snow has to forge the path. It's quite difficult for this first person, but others will follow on the path, and it gets progressively easier with each person.

Forming a habit is like forging that initial path. At first, it is hard and cumbersome. You have to watch your feet and concentrate on your steps. As the path gets more and more worn, it's hard *not* to take the path. Suppose the initial person forging the path through the snow chose to create that new path rather than take another seemingly easier path. Maybe she knew from the outset the new path would be the best path.

Perhaps she knew she'd encounter dangerous animals on an easier path. Or she knew this harder new path would lead her to a warm cottage with a delicious meal awaiting.

So consider this idea: what if you set up your habit work so you'd encounter wild beasts if you failed to clear your new path, and you'd find a warm cottage and hot meal at the end of your habit work (metaphorically speaking)?

Negative and Positive Feedback

We've all attempted and failed at creating a new habit or changing an old habit many times in our lives. One of the main reasons we fail has to do with the negative feedback that accompanies change. In this context, negative feedback is something that's uncomfortable, painful, or difficult. Or it's a situation in which we get criticized or experience a bad feeling rather than a good one. Exercise, for example, contains inherent negative feedback, as it is more difficult and uncomfortable than sitting on the couch. In this same example, positive feedback might include that satisfying feeling you get from completing a run, compliments from friends and family that you look thinner or healthier, or the thrill of seeing the number on the scale dropping.

Habit creation fails because the negative feedback from performing the new habit often outweighs the positive feedback. It's easier to skip the habit than suffer the negative feedback. So how do you overcome this problem? When negative feedback outweighs positive feedback, habit change fails. To make the habit change successful, positive feedback has to outweigh negative feedback. The solution—increase positive feedback and/or decrease negative feedback until the ratio favors success with the habit.

You must put obstacles along all other possible paths so that it's difficult to go anywhere but the path you want to take—your new habit. You want to make the path as enticing as possible, so you desire to take it. You can design your habit change work so it's harder to quit than to stick to the habit. Here are some ideas for designing your habit work with positive and negative feedback.

Increase Positive Feedback

Some habits have immediate positive feedback, but often the positive feedback is delayed. It takes time to lose weight. It takes months to finish writing a book. A long delay in positive feedback causes many people to fail, because in those critical first few weeks, they need reinforcement and positive feelings to keep them motivated.

If immediate positive feedback isn't built into your particular habit, find ways to create it. In fact, the more positives, the better.

Add as many of the examples below (and others you can think of) as possible to increase your chances of success.

- Create a vision board about your new habit and how your life will look once you create the habit. Hang the board where you can see it every day.

- Create a log or journal where you write down your daily habit work, so you see the results immediately and feel happy with your success.

- Ask your partner or another family member or friend to give you daily words of support and praise when you complete your habit.

- Participate in a Facebook group or habits forum where you can receive positive reinforcement from others going through the same thing.

- Join an in-person group, like a book club, a running club, a meet-up, etc., for support and camaraderie.

- Stay on track with your daily reward system, and try to find a reward you have a positive craving for.

- Email or talk to people about your habit change, giving them daily updates. If people expect the daily updates, you will feel motivated to do your habit so you can tell people about it.

- Blog about it and share your habit successes and efforts with your readers who will likely be encouraging and positive.

Decrease Negative Feedback

Take a moment to list the negative feedback for your particular habit. For exercise, it could be the extra energy required or the pain of the exercise. For meditating, it might be the discomfort of sitting still and quieting your mind. Then brainstorm ways you can reduce these negatives.

- For exercise, reduce discomfort by starting small, stretching first, or icing after exercise.

- If meditation is your habit, get a comfortable pillow or begin with a guided meditation audio to help you focus.

- If decluttering is your habit, and you find it boring, turn on great music to enjoy while working.

- For eating more veggies, find delicious recipes to enhance the flavor of the veggies you're adding.

- If learning a new language is your habit, find the most fun language-learning software available.

Really brainstorm all the ways you can make your habit more enjoyable and less painful. When I first started running, I would run on a path by the river, which was so beautiful I couldn't wait to get out there, even though running was hard and painful.

Increase Negative Feedback for Skipping the Habit

You want to make it hard not to perform the habit—really, really hard. So to do that, create a lot of negativity and pain for yourself for not doing the habit.

- If you join a forum or group, provide regular updates on your progress. If you fail, you face the embarrassment of admitting it to everyone.

- Ask a spouse/partner or coach or trainer to nag you about your habit, if you don't perform it.

- Offer to pay someone or to donate money to a group every time you miss your habit. Make it a large enough sum to hurt if you fail.

- Create some other unpleasant consequences, if you fail at your habit and announce them publicly.

- Don't allow yourself to do something you really enjoy until you complete your habit.

I'm sure you can think of many others—get creative!

Decrease Positive Feedback for Skipping the Habit

What tempts you to avoid your habit today? Give this some thought, and then decrease those positive things.

- If you're trying to exercise, the positive of skipping it is strong, because you'd rather relax and enjoy time at home. So reduce the relaxation and comforts of home. Clean your oven and make the house smell terrible. Turn on annoying music or make the temperature uncomfortable in the house.

- If you're trying to eat more vegetables, the positive feedback for not eating them is the ability to eat something you like that isn't as healthy. So remove those items from your home and make your food choices include more veggie options.

- If you're trying to wake up early, there is, of course, the positive feedback that comes from sleeping in. Set up multiple alarms all around your room. Have people give you wake-up calls, so you can't sleep. Set up an early morning meeting or business call.

- If you're trying to declutter, but you really just want to sit and watch TV, pull out some of your closet clutter and put it on your couch or bed so you can't sit down and relax.

The bottom line is that you want to arrange your life so it's harder and more uncomfortable to skip your habit than it is to perform it. Brainstorm as many positive and negative feedback situations as you can. Ask friends or family to help you create ideas to support your habit work. This can be a fun exercise that will pay off in a strong, automatic habit in just a few weeks.

If you are serious about creating a new habit, do whatever you can to get out of your own way. Create the optimal conditions to ensure you perform your habit every day, and remove as many temptations to avoid it as possible. This might seem like an unnecessary step, but a little bit of planning goes a long way.

Reminder: Be sure you complete your Sticky Habits Daily Habit Reporting Form and report to your accountability group.

Chapter 15:
How to Make
Your Habit a Ritual

Let's say someone gives you a dozen beautiful roses in a glass vase. They are delivered by the local florist and left at your front door. The day you receive them, you're excited and moved by the beauty of the flowers and the gesture of the giver. Then every day for the next week, you receive another dozen roses presented the same way. They are no less beautiful, but by the third day, the excitement and novelty has worn off. By day five, you don't even bother watering them anymore, even though each dozen costs more than fifty dollars.

You've come to expect the delivery, so there's no element of surprise or interest, and you feel overwhelmed by the upkeep of all these costly flowers. They don't seem so beautiful any longer. You feel guilty and bored at the same time. But let's say another suitor is a bit more creative, although not as wealthy. He shows up at your door, rings the bell, and leaves a single red rose with an unsigned note.

The next day, he ties a beautiful batch of balloons to your mailbox, still without identifying himself. On day three, he scatters flower petals on the seat of your car, and on day four you get a phone call with a singing telegram. Every day, it is something unique, thoughtful, and creative. Although none of the gestures are expensive or over-the-top, you wake up feeling excited about this new ritual in your life and the way this person is expressing himself. What will you get? Who is it? Where will you find it? The giver too finds delight in uncovering new ways to share his feelings.

Novelty, creativity, interest, and beauty keep us engaged and inspired. Sameness and repetition bore us, even when something is initially fun and exciting. It's hard to keep your habit work exciting, especially when it's something like writing or meditating. There's only so much you can do to jazz up these habits, and eventually your efforts wear thin and grow boring. However, there is a way to keep your habit work more engaging as part of your daily routine—if you come to view your habit as a ritual.

I've learned through creating my own habits that my choices and actions need to be steeped in purpose. This adds power and motivation for me. Though the word "ritual" has a religious meaning, it also suggests something ceremonial, spiritual, and meaningful. If I focus on the ritual of my actions, they aren't just a means to an end, they are deeply valuable on their own. If you ritualize your habit work, you not only make the habit more purposeful, but also you find ways to celebrate every action that comprises your habit. Putting on your running shoes is celebrated. Grabbing your water bottle is celebrated. Stretching and breathing deeply is celebrated. Every step is celebrated—perhaps with a mantra or a song or simply the sound of feet hitting pavement.

Your habit isn't something to "get through." It's a series of small rituals to be celebrated, leading you toward your ultimate goal (of health, fitness, a completed book, a new language, etc.). Here are some rituals I've developed about different habits. Perhaps they will spark an idea for your making a ritual of your habit.

Rituals and Habits

Wake-Up Ritual (Habit: Gratitude Practice)

When I awaken, I begin the day with gratitude. I spend a few minutes in bed thinking about all my blessings. Then I set the tone for the day by thinking of three things I will accomplish today that will make me feel happy and fulfilled. Then once I stand up, I take a minute to stretch my body.

Sustenance Ritual (Habit: Eating More Fruits and Vegetables)

I like that word "sustenance." It packs so much more meaning than "food" or "diet." We eat to sustain our bodies, which house our unique selves. Eating can and should be pleasurable, as long as the food provides healthy sustenance. There are so many reasons for making poor food choices, so I find the ritual of writing down what I eat keeps me accountable to caring for my body in a way that sustains it rather than harms it. I keep a notebook in my kitchen and write down everything I eat. Writing as a mindful exercise enforces awareness of my food choices.

Workspace Ritual (Habit: Clearing My Desk)

A clean workspace removes distractions, clears your mind, removes the low-level anxiety of clutter, and fosters creativity. Taking a moment to clear your space and create a clean desk says you respect yourself enough to allow time for a better work environment. I mindfully clear my desk before I begin my first project of the day.

Work Ritual (Habit: Increased Productivity)

Before I begin a work activity (writing, coaching, research, etc.), I take a moment to remind myself why I'm doing this. Sometimes it is to connect with people. Sometimes it's to serve. Sometimes it's as basic as an action that will produce income—but that can be fun and fulfilling. If I have a task or project that feels meaningless (that is, paying bills, clearing out my email, etc.), sometimes I dedicate the project to someone I love. It makes it feel more substantive for me.

Focus Ritual (Habit: Prioritizing in the Morning)

I try really hard to focus on the task at hand. It's difficult sometimes because I work from home, and there are frequent distractions. Once I determine my top priorities for the day, I isolate one small task, and finish it within an allotted time without getting up, looking at email, etc. The clean desk really helps with this.

Moving around Ritual (Habit: Movement Break during Work)

Since 90 percent of my work is done at my computer, I try to make sure I give my body a break from sitting and staring at the monitor. I give my eyes a break from the monitor by looking outside for a few minutes every hour or so. Also I get up and stretch, walk around the house, run in place—something to move my body. I try to switch it up. I'm more productive in the mornings, so around 4:00 or 5:00 in the afternoon, I usually take a break to ride my bike or do some form of real exercise.

Drink Water Ritual (Habit: Drinking More Water)

After I have my coffee in the morning, I keep a glass of water on my desk all day. I refill it when I take my moving around break. I visualize the water moving through my body and keeping me energized. Staying hydrated keeps my mind alert and manages hunger.

Weights before Shower/Bed Ritual (Habit: Toning My Arms/Legs)

My pattern is to work a few hours in the morning before I shower. It's nice to have that luxury working from home. I keep a set of hand weights in my bathroom, and before I get in the shower, I do three sets of lunges or squats interspersed with three sets of bicep curls or tricep work. I switch this up and try to complete my sets before the water gets warm. This takes about five minutes. Before I go to bed, I do another five-minute routine of some kind for my arms and legs and/or abs.

Light a Candle and Read Ritual (Habit: Read Instead of TV before Bed)

This ritual incorporates so many lovely things. First, I recently bought a featherbed topper for my mattress. Climbing into bed feels like being wrapped in a marshmallow. I've tried to stop watching TV at night in my bed. Instead I keep a good book going all the time. I light a jasmine or lavender candle on my bedside table while reading. Simply heaven.

Think about how it feels to have a new baby who wakes you up in the middle of the night. You know you have to get up to feed the baby, even though it's hard and you're exhausted. You can either do it quickly with your mind on other things, rushing through to simply get it done so you can go back to bed—or you can stare in the baby's eyes, take your time feeding him or her, and enjoy the time together even though you feel tired.

If you're committed to your habit work, find a way to ritualize it. Make it a special part of your day. Dedicate your actions to someone you love. Create a beautiful environment. Find creative ways to celebrate your habit. View it as part of a bigger purpose for your life. As you can see, your habit work doesn't have to be boring or empty. It's often just a matter of shifting your perception of your habit and what it means to you.

Reminder: Be sure you complete your Sticky Habits Daily Habit Reporting Form and report to your accountability group.

Chapter 16:
Asking for Support and
Dealing with Negativity

Aside from the positive benefits of the habit itself, your success at forming a habit yields a tremendous amount of self-confidence and positive feeling. The sense of achievement is tremendously satisfying and provides the momentum to create even more new habits. When you realize you can overcome your own internal and external obstacles, you feel you can achieve just about anything.

One obstacle you might not anticipate is the reaction of the people closest to you. Hopefully, your friends and family will be supportive and encouraging of your new habit. If it is a small, personal habit like flossing your teeth or drinking more water, then the odds are good that it won't cause a ripple among those close to you. However, sometimes our habit creation can upset those near and dear to us for a variety of reasons.

Some Common Causes of Negative Reactions

Change

Most people resist change, even if it's good change. When you disrupt the status quo, it can throw people a curve and cause discomfort. If everything is sailing along smoothly, why rock the boat? Even if your habit doesn't impact anyone else, just making a change can feel like an affront.

Inconvenience

If your habit can potentially impact another person's schedule or routine, then you will likely meet some pushback, either overtly or covertly. "You're going to meditate instead of fixing my breakfast?" "Do you have to buy all of this gross health food?" "Can't you run later? I want to have dinner." Your new habit may require those close to you to make life adjustments or sacrifices, and sometimes they won't like it.

Threat

As you improve yourself for the better and become more confident and disciplined, some people will feel threatened by your success. Your accomplishments will shine the spotlight on their own perceived failures or inadequacies. It's human nature to feel jealous or intimidated when a friend is successful, but mature people manage these feelings and translate them into encouragement and hopefully self-motivation. For some, those threatening feelings make their way to the surface, and they act on them. They find subtle or not-so-subtle ways to undermine your efforts. If they can derail you, they won't feel so bad about their own failures.

Good Intentions

There may be some genuine people close to you who want to help, protect you from failure, or manage your expectations. Perhaps they have watched you tackle a habit before unsuccessfully, and they don't want to see you hurt or disheartened. Or maybe they have a method for success they feel is better than what you are doing. They offer their input, opinions, and advice in a well-meaning way, but it has the unintended result of impairing your efforts.

You will likely encounter one or more of these scenarios within your circle of family and friends as you create new habits. So how can you manage these situations so they don't hinder your germinating habit? Here are some ideas for dealing with naysayers and well-intentioned friends.

Prepare Them

Well before you begin working on your habit, sit down with those closest to you (particularly anyone who lives with you), and tell them what you are planning. Ask for their support and encouragement, and request specifically what you need from them. Let them know how their lives might be disrupted or altered, and jointly come to an agreement about how these disruptions can be managed. Get their buy-in and manage their expectations before you launch your new routine. If you've already begun, it's not too late. Communication will make a huge difference in their support of you.

Set Boundaries

If well-intentioned or not-so-well-intentioned people want to offer unneeded advice, negative input, or subtle digs, kindly but firmly ask them to stop. Remind them you need to stay focused on your plan, and ask them again to support you with words of encouragement. Do this several times until they get the message.

Remove Yourself

During the period you are beginning your new habit, you may need to stay away from specific people who will undermine your efforts. Those who feel threatened by your habit are the ones you'll need to stay away from for a while. Eventually, they will get used to the "new you," but while you are focused on the challenges of habit formation, you don't need to expend energy on negative encounters.

Be Flexible

If your habit requires your spouse, partner, or family members to adjust their own lives, you'll need to be flexible if they get frustrated. You may need to alter your plan to make it more manageable for those around you. Sit down with them and renegotiate your habit plan. Don't use this as an excuse to give up. If they are loving and supportive, they will help you find a way to make it work for everyone.

Suggest a Partnership

Ask your spouse, partner, family member, or friend to join you in your new habit. This might be a great opportunity to bring you closer in a mutual effort that is positive and healthy. Working with someone is far easier than working against them. They may say no, but it never hurts to ask. If they don't want to join you, don't take it personally. Making the decision to commit to a new habit is hard, as you know!

It's possible you may encounter strong resistance from someone close to you. This is particularly hard if it's your spouse or romantic partner. Your new habit might shine a light on some real differences between you, which can be frightening and detrimental to your relationship. If you experience this situation, get the support of a counselor or coach to help you navigate through the issues that your new habit is inflaming.

This might be a period of growth and renewal in your relationship. When you come to these crossroads, you need to address them, rather than plowing ahead with your habit or giving up on it. If one partner in the relationship is sacrificing something essential, the relationship can't thrive. Nor can the new habit. Habit formation doesn't happen in isolation. You need the support of those closest to you to be successful. Prepare them for your upcoming changes, and prepare yourself for their potential reactions. That way, you can create a positive environment that encourages success and allows you to focus your time and energy on the work of creating your new habit.

Reminder: Be sure you complete your Sticky Habits Daily Habit Reporting Form and report to your accountability group.

Chapter 17:
Dealing with Disruptions

No one can stick to the same routine day in and day out, week in and week out. Life gets in the way. We get sick, unexpected work projects disrupt things, there are family emergencies, deaths of loved ones, injuries, vacations, work trips, children's illnesses, special occasions, visitors from out of town, holiday parties . . . the list goes on and on.

There will always be something that comes up to disrupt our routines. Disruption in routines can disrupt our habit work. How can we stick with an exercise habit, for example, when we get sick or injured? When we have a funeral to go to, or we're on a trip? How do we stick to our writing or guitar-playing habit when we are swamped with a huge work project and have no time during a particular week? These disruptions aren't easy, and they are one of the biggest reasons people stop working on their habits. How do we deal with disruptions so we can stay on track with our habit change? Here are some thoughts.

Dealing with Disruptions

Don't Catastrophize about Interruptions

We must accept there will be interruptions and not allow this to overwhelm or discourage us. Too often we feel guilty because we didn't perform the habit, or we feel discouraged because we aren't disciplined enough. Try to let go of these feelings, and don't allow them get in your way. Changes always happen, and we must learn to deal with them. Disruptions don't have to become the end of the world, or even the end of your habit creation.

Anticipate the Interruptions

If you know you're going on a trip, there's a big project coming up, or a holiday or other special occasion around the corner, plan ahead for these events. Determine in advance when to do your exercise habit while traveling. Carve out some extra time during busy work weeks. Sometimes a change in routine means you don't have the trigger connected to your habit, so find a temporary trigger (a wake-up call in a hotel, returning to your hotel room after a business meeting, changing your habit from morning to evening, and using a bedtime habit as a trigger).

Do the Habit Partially

If the disruption means you can't do the whole habit, see if you can do part of it. For exercise, you might not do your entire routine, but if you can do a little piece of it, it'll help you feel like you have continuity. If your habit is writing, even writing a paragraph is better than not doing the habit at all. Just perform one or two minutes of your habit instead of your usual amount of time.

Resume When You Can

If you are disrupted and can't do your habit, don't worry about it. Just resume the habit as soon as you can. It's not a big deal to have disruptions—what matters most is the long run, not the short term. So get back on the horse as soon as possible.

Learn and Improve

If you fail for any reason, again, it's not a big deal. Figure out what caused the failure, and learn from that. Improve on the next attempt at your habit change. Each time you try again, you get better and discern how to overcome the obstacles of previous attempts.

Keep in mind disruptions are inevitable. If you can plan for them or foresee any that might be down the road, then modify your habit work accordingly. If disruptions occur unexpectedly, do what you can to continue with your habit work or a portion of your habit. If you miss some time with your habit, just get back to it as soon as possible.

If you miss more than a day, remember to go back to the amount of practice time from the previous week to help you stay on track.

Reminder: Be sure you complete your Sticky Habits Daily Habit Reporting Form and report to your accountability group.

Chapter 18:
Staying Flexible during
Habit Creation

You've been thinking about adopting this new habit for months. You've tried a few times and haven't been successful. Now you've taken the big step of reading this book to learn habit creation skills. You've paid money, and you're determined to make it stick this time. At this point, you have developed a detailed plan for your habit creation work. You've chosen one habit to focus on, made sure it's simple, and created a system of support and accountability. All the action steps are defined. You are in a good frame of mind, working diligently on your habit, and feeling like you are headed in the right direction. Just keep this up, and the habit will become automatic any day now.

Then one day, something shifts. For some reason, the plan doesn't feel right, or something isn't working. You're doing everything right, but you know something needs to be different. How can this be happening now when you planned everything so carefully? With habit creation, as with life in general, things change. As you begin a journey, you might anticipate a linear path to your destination, but often the discoveries we make along the way lead us off the beaten path.

You can resist this internal nudging and press on, but it's likely your intuition is telling you something important, if you allow yourself to listen. This nudging can take the form of obstacles thrown in your path—an illness, injury, or disruptive life events. Sometimes we come to realize what we thought we wanted, or the way we planned to get it, isn't what we really wanted after all. We simply don't know what we don't know until we encounter it.

For example . . .

- You want to lose five pounds and create a habit of running daily. Then you realize you hate running and would rather do something else, like swimming or biking.

- You've committed to eating more vegetables daily, but the sudden diet change is making you feel bloated and uncomfortable.

- You set up a system of accountability, but it's beginning to feel intrusive and uncomfortable.

- You've devised a great plan for cleaning your house, but now you realize you really want to get rid of some stuff rather than clean it.

- You planned to do your yoga first thing when you wake up, but you feel you need to shower first to be in the right frame of mind.

- You've committed to writing every day, but you really miss spending time with your kids in the morning, since you've replaced that time with writing.

Sometimes you have to go partially down a path before you realize you need to alter your course. That doesn't mean you've failed in your habit or that you're looking for excuses to stop. It just means you need to stay flexible and adaptable to your changing needs or circumstances. Altering our plans midway is disruptive for most of us and downright painful for those who can't stand deviation. However, if the change in plan ultimately helps you accomplish your habit, perform it more effectively, or redirects you to another habit that serves you better, then it's well worth the disruption.

As you work on your own habit during the next few weeks, remain receptive to any shifts and changes you notice in yourself. You may not always need to act on them, but give yourself the room to make an intelligent decision about whether or not they are useful. Self-questioning is a great way to get to the bottom of what you want and what you need to do. Try these questions when you feel something might need to change (and write down your answers in your journal).

- What am I feeling exactly (resistance, discomfort, re-morse, frustration, etc.)?

- Why am I feeling this way?

- What could I change to make it better?

- Is this change necessary to foster my new habit?

- How much time will this add to my habit creation?

- How do I need to change or alter my habit plan?

- How will this change impact other areas of my life?

- Am I using this as an excuse to avoid my habit?

- If so, how can I prevent it from undermining my habit work?

- Will I feel better or worse if I make this shift?

Once you decide you do need to make a change, be sure to adjust your habit plan accordingly. Advise the people who are supporting you or holding you accountable. Arrange your life schedule to accommodate any changes. Determine a new trigger if necessary. You may need to rewrite your plan if the change impacts many elements of it.

Try not to use this change as a reason to give up, get frustrated, or put yourself down. It actually reflects great strength and wisdom to admit it's not working and to readjust on the fly. Changing your mind, altering your plans, and encountering unexpected situations are likely scenarios during habit creation, so expect them. Remain flexible and adaptable to the inevitable twists and turns of your journey. Go with the flow, and perhaps you may even enjoy the new opportunities that life presents along the path to your new habit.

Reminder: Be sure you complete your Sticky Habits Daily Habit Reporting Form and report to your accountability group.

Chapter 19:
Finding Your Habit Tribe

Just the fact you're reading a book on creating habits says a lot about you. It says you want a great life. You have important things you want to accomplish. It says you want to seize your dreams. As I mentioned earlier in the book, all big goals are comprised of a series of habits. Learning to master habit formation gives you the desire and motivation to keep adding positive habits to your life—and perhaps to let go of some negative habits. It's like learning to ride a bike—once you can do it, the only thing you want to do is ride all day long. And why not? Building up a suite of great habits is not only fun, it's life-changing. Think about everything you can accomplish with this new skill.

One of the things you'll notice when you become a habit warrior is that you want to hang out with other habit warriors. You seek out others who share your desire to grow and become better, more interesting, more engaged people. These are people who are passionate about life and passionate about making things happen through positive habits. Just like you.

My first encounter with a group of likeminded, passionate people was my first coaching class. I signed up for coach training, and my first teleclass was with a group of about twenty students. We each had to introduce ourselves and share our backgrounds. I met vice-presidents of human resources; psychologists; educators; business executives; and many other interesting, intuitive, highly educated, soul-seeking people. They felt like my "tribe."

I took dozens of classes (a habit I had to form) and interacted with hundreds of other students and coach instructors. With every class, with every engagement I had with peers and instructors, I felt more enthusiastic and committed to the path I had chosen and the new habits I was adopting as part of my work. The energy, creativity, and shared interest in helping people through coaching was rocket fuel for my own aspirations and motivation toward creating more habits to build my coaching practice.

When I first began my practice, I conducted small group workshops of women seeking to reinvent themselves around their newly discovered passions. Again, I was interacting with likeminded people who were seeking to grow, live passionately, and connect with others doing the same.

During the early days of my new practice, I realized I needed to market myself online. I created a basic blog, but this was a huge leap for me to tackle this pitifully simple online tool. I was so excited about the work and the people I was serving and meeting that I pushed myself to do it. I eventually did more research on blogging and registered for a blogging course where I was interacting with a brand new group of interesting, passionate people who were committed to taking action. All these goals required me to develop habits—but I was inspired to form them because of my tribe.

When you find your "tribe"—your group of habit-conscious, likeminded people—you will be compelled to pursue your goals and dreams and will find a way to make them happen. You will be supported in pushing past fear and perceived limitations. Because you have a support network of people, you'll have a wonderful pool of resources and inspiration to help you, just as you will help them. These connections are exceedingly fulfilling and satisfying.

Here are some thoughts on how you can find your tribe of habit warriors.

Find Your Tribe

Go for It

As you consider your next habit, take the step to get involved with other people who share your same interest. Sign up for a course or class; get involved in a meet-up or group; go to that conference. Put yourself in the midst of passionate people who share your interest and really engage with them. See if they feel like your tribe. Pay attention to how you feel around them—if they inspire and motivate you.

Be the Connector

Become the person who brings other passionate, habit-conscious people together. Make introductions, share ideas and information, host a workshop, create a mastermind group, look for opportunities for deeper engagement to expand your network, and become the "go-to" person in your habit community who makes things happen. Don't sit back and wait. Build your own community of people who can be a support and inspiration to one another.

Be Real

The only way you will find the right tribe that really supports your habits and goals is by being real and vulnerable yourself. Be willing to share who you are, what your goals are, and where you need support and help. The key to great communities of passionate, likeminded people is authenticity. Allow yourself to be enthusiastic, open, and adopt the mindset of a lifelong learner who is always willing to learn and grow.

Avoid Naysayers

It's inevitable when you become passionate about your habit and excited about your achievements that you'll encounter people who want to criticize or undermine your enthusiasm. They may tell you why it won't work, why you don't deserve it, what you are doing wrong, or how you are inconveniencing them. Do your best to stay away from these people, or at least attempt to block their negativity from your psyche.

Spend most of your time with people who are positive, excited, and action-oriented. Find people who want to mentor you rather than push you down.

Don't Hibernate

Whatever you do, don't get so entrenched in the details of your habit work that you neglect to find and engage with your tribe of passionate people. This is so easy to do, especially if your habit requires isolation (like writing or meditating). You must make yourself get out there and engage. Making connections with your tribe can make a real difference in propelling you toward success and enthusiasm to tackle new positive habits. These are the people who will inspire you, motivate you, and serve as accountability partners and resources for ideas and support.

One of the rewards of creating new habits is the joy you feel in sharing your experiences and accomplishments with others. Your tribe can become your new best friends. In fact, you might find a future business partner among them. You might find the love of your life. You might have new opportunities for adventure or travel. Don't allow your new habit to be a private affair. Get out there and connect so you can squeeze the most enjoyment from your lifetime habit skills.

Reminder: Be sure you complete your Sticky Habits Daily Habit Reporting Form and report to your accountability group.

Chapter 20:
The Importance of
Keystone Habits

Now that you've learned the basic skills of habit creation, you need to consider choosing a keystone habit as you continue your habit forming work in the future. Keystone habits are particular habits that make success in many other aspects of life far easier, regardless of the circumstances you face. These habits unlock a cascade of positive behavior changes with far less effort than establishing a single habit from the ground up.

According to Charles Duhigg in his book *The Power of Habit*, research shows we all have a few keystone habits that transform other areas of our lives. They trigger a chain of internal events that kickstart the willpower and motivation to achieve other goals. When you strategically create a keystone habit and build from it, you create the foundation for a string of small wins. These small wins build momentum and positive feedback, which are crucial to effective habit change. It doesn't matter how big or small your keystone habit is—what matters is that you follow through with it every day and use it as a platform to build other positive habits.

Two keystone habits Charles Duhigg highlights in his book are exercise and food journaling. Here's what he says about exercise:

> When people start habitually exercising, even as infrequently as once a week, they start changing other, unrelated patterns in their lives, often unknowingly. Typically people who exercise start eating better and becoming more productive at work. They smoke less and show more patience with colleagues and family. They use their credit cards less frequently and say they feel less stressed. It's not completely clear why . . . "Exercise spills over," said James Prochaska, a University of Rhode Island researcher. "There's something about it that makes other good habits easier" (p. 109).

When you invest time and energy in exercise, you inspire yourself to make other beneficial changes in your life without consciously planning to do so. You're motivated to support your exercise habit with other health-affirming behaviors, such as eating more vegetables or meditating.

Food journaling is another keystone habit Duhigg highlights. When you focus on weight loss, keeping track of food intake increases the intrinsic reward of good behavior by creating the extrinsic reward of seeing your food consumption documented. Duhigg explains how researchers of a large weight-loss study were surprised to see just how effective it was, and how it influenced other behaviors.

> It was hard at first [writing down everything one day per week]. The subjects forgot to carry their food journals, or would snack and not note it. Slowly, however, people started recording their meals once a week—and sometimes, more often . . . Eventually, it became a habit. Then, something unexpected happened. The participants started looking at their entries and finding patterns they didn't know existed. Some noticed they always seemed to snack at about 10 A.M., so they began keeping an apple or banana on their desks for midmorning munchies. Others started using their journals to plan future menus, and when dinner rolled around, they ate the healthy meal they had written down, rather than junk food from the fridge (p. 120).

The chore of recording food was difficult at first—as all new habits are. But researchers found that six months into the study, people who kept food records daily lost twice as much weight as everyone else. Because of their heightened awareness, they were primed to make additional positive changes to their behavior.

Exercise and food journaling are just two examples of keystone habits, and they're by no means simple to implement. But they've been shown to serve as catalysts that cause widespread shifts in your life. In an article posted online at *A Life of Productivity* Duhigg suggests there are three defining characteristics of keystone habits.

1. Keystone habits give you "numerous, small senses of victory." Pay attention to habits and routines that provide you with a pattern of these small wins. According to Duhigg, the positive impact of these small habits is tremendous—greater than the benefit of the habit itself.

2. Keystone habits are "the soil from which other habits [grow]." Keystone habits aren't just any new habit, like flossing your teeth. They are the foundation from which other positive habits can grow. If your keystone habit is meditation, for example, you might grow the habit of proactive, open communication with your spouse or partner as a result.

3. Keystone habits give you energy and confidence to do more. Duhigg recommends we remain mindful of "moments when excellence—or change, or perseverance, or some other virtue—seems to become contagious. Keystone habits are powerful because they change our sense of self and our sense of what is possible." Keystone habits are the gifts that keep on giving. They provide you with an infectious drive to be better and do more long after you complete your habit routine.

In addition to exercise and food journaling, here are some other keystone habits to consider creating.

- Eating family dinners together habitually has been shown to give children an edge with homework skills, better grades, confidence, and emotional control.

- Making your bed in the morning is correlated to more productivity, a sense of well-being, and budgeting skills.

- The habit of visualization when applied to a desired outcome (better performance in sports, for example) leads to habits that support increased performance.

- The habit of positive thinking creates an attitude of confidence and energy that promotes many other positive habits.

- Planning your goals and priorities the night before, for the following day, encourages commitment and follow-through on specific actions that are productive and positive.

Ultimately, you must decide what the best keystone habits are for you. You may have an idea from past experience in attempting a habit and how it triggered other positive behaviors for you. Or you may need to work on a few habits before you land on your keystone. Whatever you do, don't neglect to look for it. Keystone habits are life-changing, and identifying these habits that matter most will create widespread shifts in every aspect of your life.

Reminder: Be sure you complete your Sticky Habits Daily Habit Reporting Form and report to your accountability group.

Chapter 21:
Your Return on a
Yearly Habit Investment

It may seem obvious, but if you perform a small habit over and over again, the benefits accrue tremendously over time. We all know this, but not everyone recognizes the power of it and puts it to use. Your habit investment will pay you back in large returns by this time next year. And next year really isn't that far away. If you put just five dollars a day into an investment fund with 6 percent interest, at the end of twenty years, you'd have nearly $70,000 and closer to $90,000, if you make 8 percent. If you invest eight dollars a day, now you're talking about $140,000 or so. You can see how small savings add up over time.

This same principle applies to habits. Let's review a few examples.

- If you spend just a few minutes a day studying a new language, by the end of a year, you'll have learned enough to get by to speak the language.

- If you do a few pushups every day, by the end of a year, you'll be able to do dozens of pushups and be much stronger.

- If you write just a couple of hundred words a day, by the end of the year, you'll have enough for a full book.

Small efforts add up over time and can make a huge difference in your life. The benefits include more than just the accumulation of the small efforts—there's interest accrued as well in the form of side benefits. Exercising a little each day makes you healthier and provides stress relief. Learning a new language opens doors to meeting new people, job opportunities, and travel. Mastering any new skills or positive behaviors makes you feel more confident and capable.

Sometimes it helps to see in writing exactly how a year's worth of positive habits can change your life by the end of the year. Here are some examples of how to transform various parts of your life with a year of small habits.

Small Habits, Big Transformations

Saving Money

As I mentioned in the example before, a little savings can go a long way. You can save for something specific, like a trip, or save to get your finances in order. If you aren't saving, start by cutting out one or two small daily expenses (like Starbucks specialty coffees or dinner out each week, for example), and instead set up automatic transfers each week or every payday to your savings account. Once you have a small emergency fund, pay off debt. Once you've paid off most of your debt, start investing. Your finances will improve immensely with time.

Losing Weight

Substitute one high-fat, high-calorie food item you eat regularly for one lower-fat, lower-calorie item that's much better for you. For example, rather than having a bagel and cream cheese for breakfast, substitute that for a bowl of oatmeal with raisins and walnuts. You'll save about 200 calories a day. If that's the only change you make in your diet, you'll be twenty pounds lighter next year. Add walking thirty minutes a day, and that takes off another ten pounds a year.

Waking Up Earlier

This is an advanced habit skill, but one that can make a big difference. Try waking a few minutes earlier tomorrow—7:25 instead of 7:30. Wake up at 7:25 for a week (using the Sticky Habits Method), and then reduce it by another five minutes the next week, and so on. In fewer than six months, you'll be waking up two hours earlier, if that's your goal. It happens so gradually, you'll never feel like you're waking earlier. Don't try to wake up a lot earlier, like thirty to sixty minutes, when you begin, or you'll be bound to fail.

Writing

If you want to create a writing habit, start by writing two sentences or about twenty words. Do that for a week. Then write three or four sentences the next week. This sounds ridiculously easy, so most people will ignore this advice. But this time next year, you could be up to a habit of 1,000 words a day or more. You could have a book, a blog, or a course created in a year.

Communicating with Your Spouse or Partner

Sit with your spouse or partner for five minutes a day and share the experiences of your day. The next week, add another five minutes to share what you love about your partner. Then work up to a fifteen–twenty-minute time when you share, express love, and create a vision for your relationship together. By the end of the year, your relationship will be stronger, more open, and more loving. And you'll be on the way to making your vision real.

Learning an Instrument

Find online beginner's instruction for an instrument that interests you. For the first week, practice for five minutes a day. Work up to your desired practice time (thirty to sixty minutes) following the Sticky Habits Method. In a year, you will have mastered the basics of the instrument.

Meditating

Meditation has been proven through many, many studies to improve your health, reduce stress, and increase productivity and creativity. Begin with just three minutes of mediation, maybe using a guided meditation online to help you. Each week, add another minute to your meditation time. By the end of the year, you can work up to nearly an hour of meditation, which will have an amazing positive impact on all areas of your life.

Decluttering

Just declutter one drawer, shelf, or small closet a day. Or tackle one small part of a room for just five minutes. In a year, your house will feel roomy, organized, and less stressful.

Self-Improvement

Find an online, self-study course that will improve your skills at work or in some other area of your life. Or take an online degree program that is self-paced with a comfortable deadline. Begin the working on the course for five minutes a day and continue adding time each week. Completing the course could mean a promotion, more money, or a new job by this time next year.

There are many other good habits that can profoundly impact your life in a year's time. These are just a few of the most common, positive habit choices you might consider.

However, the regular practice of *bad* habits also accrues interest during a year's time, and the results can be unpleasant or even harmful. What does checking social media on a regular basis do for you? It doesn't do anything to help you create a desirable skill, build good health, or gain useful knowledge. Surfing the net just pulls you away from useful habits you might be pursuing. Eating junk food every day is another useless habit that is a bad investment of your time and energy, as is watching too much TV, complaining regularly, or drinking too much alcohol. These are just a few examples, but it's worth mindfully considering the habits you're accruing over time and how they serve you.

What we repeatedly do makes us who we are. So who will you be this time next year?

Pick the habits you want to define you. Do them repeatedly and watch them grow. Before you know it, your habit investments will pay off in life-changing returns.

Reminder: Be sure you complete your Sticky Habits Daily Habit Reporting Form and report to your accountability group.

Chapter 22:
How and When to Introduce
Your Next Habit

If you've been working steadily on your habit for the past four or five weeks, you probably feel like your first habit is automatic or nearly so. You feel ready to get started on your second habit, but how and when do you start? Hopefully with your first habit, you followed the Sticky Habits Method by starting small (with five minutes or so) and performing your habit most days (at least 85–90 percent). Your habit should be on autopilot at this point, and, if that's the case, you're ready to put the first habit on the back burner and focus on another new habit.

However, you can't completely forget about the first habit. Even after a month, you can backslide if you forget your original habit for a few days. Stay consistent with the first habit, even as you begin your new habit. Remember, you created this first habit for a good reason, and you want this positive behavior to remain in your life. The more consistent you are with the first habit, the stronger it will become, and you'll be mentally tougher to pursue the next habit.

If you weren't consistent with the first habit in the initial thirty days, you're not ready to move on. You can drop this habit if you want and start a new one, but since you have some momentum with it, I suggest you keep it going until you master it. Either way, you can learn from what went wrong, and plan for improvement the next time. Don't beat yourself up if you weren't successful. Now you have the habit-creation skills, and you can start again with the first habit or move on to the next, ready to beat the obstacles that stopped you the first time. You're wiser now, so you're more likely to succeed if you maintain focus.

If you want to move on to your next habit, remember you're not a habit master just yet. You still need to start with just five minutes and work on a positive habit rather than beating a negative habit. Practice this simple Sticky Habits Method for at least three to four easy habits before moving on to harder habits, like dropping a negative habit or tackling thinking habits. Mastering seven to eight easy, positive habits is even better. You're working on a tough skill, so practice, practice, practice. Get lots of experience, and then tackle the tough ones.

Once you begin it, give your second habit full focus, as you did with the first. Be conscious of performing the habit every single time you perform your trigger. If your first habit is really solid and works with the timing of your second, you might consider using the first habit as the trigger for the second. You can stack small habits this way where each new habit becomes the trigger for the next. However, only do this if your first habit is really strong, and it's something you do every single day. Your trigger for the new habit must be regular and predictable. Otherwise, choose a different trigger that works with your new habit.

Your second habit is going to take a lot of energy and commitment—almost as much as the first one did. Don't take it lightly just because you've had one successful habit change. Follow the Sticky Habits Method exactly as you did with the first habit—having a week before you begin your habit for preparation and planning. Establish your trigger, your reward, and your accountability and support systems. Start small with five minutes and build slowly. Consider any possible roadblocks or difficulties with your habit and create a backup plan.

Harder habits include dropping bad habits and tackling habits that aren't daily—they might have triggers that come several times a week, or only one weekday or weekend, or only with certain people. Even harder habits are mental habits, such as overcoming negative thinking, being judgmental, or getting angry. Tackle these only after you're good at habits—maybe after tackling five to eight easier habits. If you feel you're ready to begin your next habit, set aside a week right now to begin your planning and preparation. Congratulations! You've learned the Sticky Habits Method, you have one amazing new habit under your belt, and you're on your way to becoming a habit ninja!

Reminder: Be sure you complete your Sticky Habits Daily Habit Reporting Form and report to your accountability group.

Conclusion and Next Steps

Congratulations, you are now the proud owner of a shiny, brand new habit. If you faltered with your habit work, don't give up on yourself or on learning the Sticky Habits Method. Just begin again, following the same steps outlined in this book. Creating a small, new, positive habit is the easiest kind of habit to form, so hop back on and get started.

The main goal of this book has been to help you learn the method so you can apply it to any habit change you'd like in the future. Now you have the skills to do just that, even if you haven't completed your work on your first habit. So what's next, now that you've finished this book?

Four Things You Need to Do

1. Continue building the habit skill.

This means repeating the method with a simple, new, positive habit with a daily trigger—just as you did over the past few weeks. Do this at least twice more before moving on, so you really have the skills of habit creation well-established. You can start on new habits every six weeks or so, especially once the habit feels automatic, and you don't need reminders or accountability. You'll need to maintain it, but it won't be hard.

2. Tackle slightly tougher skills.

The next level of skill would be new, positive habits with variable triggers—once a week, only on weekends or weekdays, every other day, or at unpredictable times. Maybe you want to develop the habit of running every other day, or maybe you want to wake up an hour earlier just on weekdays. Obviously this is harder because you're not performing the habit every day.

3. Take on thinking skills.

Thinking skills involve changing negative thought habits and replacing them with positive thought habits. Quite often changing a thinking habit can be a keystone habit, positively impacting your ability to form other habits. Working on thinking habits is similar to dropping a bad habit that has preexisting triggers that compel you to perform the bad habit (for example, drinking coffee might trigger smoking a cigarette). The preexisting triggers for negative thoughts are even more subtle and require focused awareness to notice them.

Bad thinking habits tend to come at variable times, with many different triggers. Start by tracking the times your negatives thoughts are triggered and what the triggers are. Then focus on replacing the old thinking pattern with a new positive thought whenever the trigger happens. For example, you might find you have negative thoughts while taking a shower. Notice them and intentionally change the negative thoughts into a positive. Try placing a rubber band on your wrist to remind you to stay aware of your negative thought habits, especially if your triggers are variable. It takes a lot of concentration to change a thinking habit, but otherwise, the Sticky Habits Method is the same for these habits.

4. Quit a negative habit.

These are hardest habits to tackle, because they have multiple triggers, and they are so ingrained that you'll have strong urges to do the habit. It's definitely not impossible though. Start with a small, bad habit that doesn't have a physical addiction associated with it—something like nail biting or surfing the net too much. Practice with a few easier bad habits before trying to quit smoking, caffeine, drinking, or any habit that might involve unpleasant physical symptoms if you stop.

Quitting bad habits deserves a separate book, but for now realize that your bad habits are already triggered by other habits. Pay attention to the triggers and when they occur, be prepared with a replacement for your bad habit. The urge may not go away for a while, but you'll be armed with a positive behavior to put in its place.

A Final Note

All the steps of the Sticky Habits Method remain necessary and important as you continue to form habits for years to come. Don't skip them just because you've mastered a few habits already. Each step of the method plays an important role in making you more likely to succeed. Don't take habit change lightly! Although you know the skills, you have to create new neural pathways in your brain with each and every new habit. The greater the number of easy habits you master, the more skillful you will become. Once you're skillful and experienced with a few easy habits, then you can tackle slightly harder ones. Build the skill with practice, and remember you will likely fail at some habit changes. Don't get discouraged. Try to learn from each failure, adjust your actions, and get better.

In the past few weeks, you have learned a skill that will upgrade your life in so many ways. Your life will improve; you will become a more interesting, accomplished person; and your self-esteem and self-confidence will soar. Each new habit opens doors of opportunity, better relationships, greater health and well-being, and even more money. Great habits add up to an amazing life. Thank you so much for joining me for *Sticky Habits*. Wishing you a lifetime of positive habits!

Want to Learn More?

If you'd like to learn more about creating habits, please visit my blogs for more articles.

Live Bold and Bloom (www.liveboldandbloom.com)

BarrieDavenport.com
(www.barriedavenport.com)

Or check out my online course,

Sticky Habits (www.stickyhabits.com).

Did You Like *Sticky Habits*?

Thank you so much for purchasing *Sticky Habits*. I'm honored by the trust you've placed in me and my work by choosing this book to learn the skills of habit creation. I truly hope you've enjoyed it and found it useful for your life.

I'd like to ask you for a small favor. Could you please take just a minute to leave a review for this book on Amazon? This feedback will help me continue to write the kind of Kindle books that will best serve you. If you really loved the book, please let me know!

Other Books You Might Enjoy from Barrie Davenport

Emotional Abuse Breakthrough: How to Speak Up, Set Boundaries, and Break the Cycle of Manipulation and Control with Your Abusive Partner
(liveboldandbloom.com/eab-book)

Emotional Abuse Breakthrough Scripts: 107 Empowering Responses and Bondaries to Use with Your Abuser
(liveboldandbloom.com/ea-scripts)

Building Confidence: Get Motivated, Overcome Social Fear, Be Assertive, and Empower Your Life for Success
(liveboldandbloom.com/building-confidence)

Peace of Mindfulness: Everyday Rituals to Conquer Anxiety and Claim Unlimited Inner Peace
(liveboldandbloom.com/mindfulness-post)

Finely Tuned: How to Thrive as a Highly Sensitive Person or Empath
(liveboldandbloom.com/finely-tuned)

201 Relationship Questions: The Couple's Guide to Building Trust and Emotional Intimacy
(liveboldandbloom.com/201-questions)

Self-Discovery Questions: 155 Breakthrough Questions to Accelerate Massive Action
(liveboldandbloom.com/questions-book)

Confidence Hacks: 99 Small Actions to Massively Boost Your Confidence
(liveboldandbloom.com/confidence-hacks)

10-Minute Declutter: The Stress-Free Habit for Simplifying Your Home
(liveboldandbloom.com/10-min-declutter)

10-Minute Digital Declutter: The Simple Habit to Eliminate Technology Overload
(liveboldandbloom.com/digital-declutter)

Declutter Your Mind: How to Stop Worrying, Relieve Anxiety, and Eliminate Negative Thinking
(liveboldandbloom.com/declutter-mind)

The 52-Week Life Passion Project: Uncover Your Life Passion
(liveboldandbloom.com/life-passion-book)

Notes

Chapter 4: Selecting a Trigger

In the book *The Power of Habit: Why We Do What We Do in Life and Business*, author Charles Duhigg discusses experiments in habit formation done with rats.

> Charles Duhigg, *The Power of Habit: Why We Do What We Do in Life and Business,* New York: Random House, 2012.

Chapter 5: Cultivating Cravings and Establishing Rewards

In a 2002 study at New Mexico State University, researchers looked at 266 people who exercised at least three times a week.

> Krystina A. Finlay, David Trafimow, and Aimee Villarreal, "Predicting Exercise and Health Behavioral Intentions: Attitudes, Subjective Norms, and Other Behavioral Determinants," *Journal of Applied Social Psychology* 32 (2002): 342–356.

Chapter 11: Your Brain and Habit Creation

Neuroplasticity is "one of the most extraordinary discoveries of the twentieth century," according to psychiatrist Norman Doidge, MD, author of *The Brain That Changes Itself.*

> See http://www.normandoidge.com/?page_id=1639.

Jeffrey Schwartz, author of *The Mind and the Brain: Neuroplasticity and the Power of Mental Force*, made an extraordinary discovery while using the therapy he developed for his patients with obsessive-compulsive disorder.

Jeffrey Schwartz and Sharon Begley, *The Mind and the Brain: Neuroplasticity and the Power of Mental Force*, New York: Harper, 2002.

A review in the *Strength and Conditioning Journal* describes how to use imagery to improve strength training.

Richter, J., J. Gilbert, and M. Baldis, "Maximizing Strength Training Performance using Mental Imagery," *Strength and Conditioning Journal* 34,5 (2012): 65–70.

Chapter 12: How Long Does It Really Take to Create a Habit?

In 1960, Dr. Maxwell Maltz published a best-selling book called *Psycho-Cybernetics* in which he discussed his observations about how long it took amputees to adjust to the loss of a limb.

Maxwell Maltz, *Psycho-Cybernetics: A New Way to Get More Living out of Life*, New York: Simon & Schuster, 1960.

His book became a blockbuster hit, selling more than thirty-five million copies.

Maxwell Maltz, *Psycho-Cybernetics, Updated and Expanded*, New York: Tarcher-Perigree, 2015, Foreword.

In a 2009 study published in the *European Journal of Social Psychology*, Phillippa Lally and her colleagues from University College London conducted more definitive research on habit creation.

Phillippa Lally, Cornelia H. M. van Jaarsveld, Henry W. W. Potts, and Jane Wardle, "How Are Habits Formed: Modeling Habit Formation in the Real World," *European Journal of Social Psychology* 40,6 (2010): 998–1009.

Chapter 14: Creating Positive and Negative Feedback

In his ebook about changing habits, blogger Scott Young (www.ScottHYoung.com/blog) describes the process of forming habits like walking home through fresh snow.

> Scott H. Young, *How to Change a Habit.* See https://www.scotthyoung.com/blog/sales-pages/how-to-change-a-habit/.

Chapter 20: The Importance of Keystone Habits

According to Charles Duhigg in his book *The Power of Habit*, research shows we all have a few keystone habits that transform other areas of our lives.

> Charles Duhigg, *The Power of Habit: Why We Do What We Do in Life and Business,* New York: Random House, 2012.

An article posted online at *A Life of Productivity* suggests there are three defining characteristics of keystone habits.

> Chris Bailey, *"3 Ways to Identify Your 'Keystone Habits,' Habits That Change Everything,* January 30,2014. See http://alifeofproductivity.com/3-ways-identify-keystone-habits-habits-set-chain-reaction-change-everything/.

42945272R00102

Made in the USA
San Bernardino, CA
12 December 2016